DARE YOUR VULNERABILITY

Harness The Power of Vulnerability, Build Resilience and Authenticity, Navigate Uncertainty, Transform Through Adversity

SEKHAR KUMAR DEY

Copyright

Dedication

To my beloved wife,

Sumita Dey

Your steadfast love and boundless patience have been my guiding light. You stood by my side through every challenge and storm, your strength lifting me when I faltered. Your unwavering support never wavered despite my temperament and the trials I brought into our lives.

You are my rock, my confidant, and my greatest blessing. This book is as much yours as mine, a testament to your incredible strength and the love that sustains me every day.

With deepest gratitude and all my love,
Sekhar Kumar Dey

How this book can help you?

"The mind is everything. What you think you become." – Buddha

"Dare Your Vulnerability" is a transformative guide designed to help readers harness the power of vulnerability for personal and professional growth. By sharing compelling stories and practical insights, this book offers a roadmap for embracing vulnerability, shifting perspectives, and cultivating emotional intelligence. Here are the key benefits that readers will gain from this book:

Chapter 1: Unconventional Wisdom: Embrace Your Truth

1. **Embrace Failure as a Learning Tool**: Failure is a stepping stone to success, as illustrated by stories like those of the Taj Mahal and Richard Branson. Learn to view setbacks as opportunities for growth and development.
2. **Challenge Conventional Wisdom:** This book encourages you to develop the ability to question accepted narratives and think independently. This leads to a deeper understanding and personal growth, empowering you to shape your path.
3. **Understand Your Unique Perspective:** By embracing your unique perspective, you can recognize the value of your viewpoint and learn to navigate life holistically.
4. **Right to Make Mistakes:** Foster growth by making independent decisions and learning from mistakes rather than unthinkingly following others' advice.

5. **Self-Belief Over Social Expectations:** Overcome societal limiting beliefs, especially those imposed on individuals with learning differences, and believe in your potential for personal success.
6. **Critique of Social Judgments:** Highlight the need for a more inclusive society and emphasize the strengths of neurodiverse individuals.
7. **Impact of Historical Actions on Present Perceptions:** Understand how past actions shape current perceptions and form nuanced opinions about historical symbols.
8. **Value of Independent Thinking:** Develop the courage to think and act independently, which will lead to authentic and fulfilling life choices.
9. **Redefining Success and Worth:** Measure success by personal growth and learning, not societal benchmarks.
10. **Power of Vulnerability:** Embrace vulnerability as a powerful tool for personal development, resilience, and self-understanding.

Chapter 2: Shifting Perspectives: Understanding the Power of Mindset

1. **Power of an Open Stance and Vulnerability**: Embrace openness and vulnerability to fuel personal growth and foster curiosity and learning.
2. **Cultivating Resilience**: Build resilience through growth across emotional, mental, spiritual, and physical realms.
3. **Leading with Curiosity:** Foster continuous learning and openness by questioning beliefs.

4. **Impact of Mindset on Success**: Adopt a growth mindset to view challenges as opportunities and foster perseverance and adaptability.
5. **Breaking Free from Limiting Beliefs**: Challenge limiting beliefs to unlock potential and achieve remarkable personal growth.
6. **Clarify Your Goals:** Define specific goals clearly and visualize success to maintain focus and motivation.
7. **Practice Mental Rehearsal:** Use mental rehearsal techniques to enhance performance and reinforce commitment to your goals.
8. **Create a Vision Board:** Keep your aspirations tangible and reinforce motivation with a vision board.
9. **Use Affirmations:** Maintain focus and boost confidence with positive affirmations.
10. **Live in the Moment:** Balance visualization with present-moment awareness to enhance clarity and effectiveness.

Chapter 3: Self-Compassion: Cultivating Emotional Intelligence for Success

1. **Emotional Intelligence (EI) Beyond IQ:** Understand the importance of EI in making wise decisions and avoiding costly mistakes.
2. **Components of EI:** Learn to navigate challenges, manage stress, and build relationships with self-awareness, self-regulation, motivation, empathy, and social skills.
3. **Self-Regulation**: Master self-regulation to control impulses and manage negative emotions.
4. **Practical Strategies:** Enhance EI with mindfulness, self-reflection, and recognizing physiological cues.

5. **Benefits of EI:** Improve decision-making, interpersonal skills, and overall well-being by developing EI.
6. **Professional and Personal Success:** Enhance resilience, social skills, and leadership effectiveness with high EI.
7. **Relationships and Communication**: Improve interpersonal relations with better empathy, conflict resolution, and communication skills.
8. **Stress Management**: Recognize and manage stress effectively to improve mental and physical well-being.
9. **Decision-Making and Motivation:** Enhance decision-making and boost intrinsic motivation with high EI.
10. **Happiness and Well-Being:** Increase life satisfaction and well-being with improved self-awareness, relationship satisfaction, and stress reduction.

Chapter 4: Rewiring Your Brain: Unraveling the Neuroscience of Change

1. **Neuroplasticity and Mindset Shifts:** Reframe thoughts and behaviors by actively rewiring your brain.
2. **Practical Strategies for Enhancing Neuroplasticity:** Strengthen neural pathways and improve cognitive flexibility with daily nutrition, adequate sleep, and mental exercises.
3. **Impact of Dopamine and Serotonin**: Balance dopamine and serotonin levels to enhance happiness and productivity.
4. **Biological Basis of Happiness:** Understand the complex interplay of biological and environmental factors in happiness.

5. **Practical Applications in Daily Life**: Optimize brain function and promote emotional resilience with mindfulness practices, a healthy lifestyle, and positive social connections.
6. **Understanding Habit Formation:** Develop good and break bad habits by understanding cues, rewards, and supportive environments.
7. **Challenges in Habit Development:** Overcome hurdles in forming good habits with small, consistent efforts.
8. **Role of Brain-Based Learning in Habit Formation:** Enhance retention and habit formation with brain-based learning techniques.
9. **Practical Strategies for Lasting Change:** Recognize triggers, replace routines, and maintain progress by tracking behavior.
10. **Creating Supportive Environments**: Foster positive habits with habit-tracking apps, clear goals, and a supportive social circle.

Chapter 5: Vulnerability: The Gateway to Resilience and Authenticity

1. **Embrace Vulnerability for Growth:** View vulnerability as a personal and professional growth catalyst.
2. **Authenticity Drives Leadership:** Build trust and create a supportive work environment with authentic leadership.
3. **Courageous Leadership:** Encourage openness and emotional exposure to empower teams and drive innovation.

4. **Resilience and Grit Matter:** Build character and prepare for workplace challenges with resilience and grit.
5. **Navigating Conflict with Vulnerability:** Facilitate understanding and resolution in relationships and conflicts by embracing vulnerability.
6. **Embrace Vulnerability:** Build trust and foster genuine connections in relationships, leadership, and personal growth with vulnerability.
7. **Choose Love Over Fear:** Transform relationships by choosing acceptance over judgment and operating from love.
8. **Leadership and Vulnerability:** Create psychological safety within teams by embracing vulnerability.
9. **Overcoming Perfectionism:** Embrace imperfection to grow, form deeper connections, and find joy in life's uncertainties.
10. **Learning from Role Models:** Learn from the stories of Brené Brown and Richard Branson to embrace vulnerability for resilience, creativity, and meaningful achievements.

"Dare Your Vulnerability" is your guide to embracing vulnerability, shifting perspectives, and cultivating emotional intelligence. This book provides the tools to navigate challenges, foster personal growth, and achieve success. Embrace your authentic self and unlock your full potential with its transformative insights.

Table of Content

Chapter 1: Unconventional Wisdom: Embrace Your Truth

1.1 My Vulnerable Stand: Case Studies of The Taj Mahal and Richard Branson

"The greatest mistake you can make is continually fearing you will make one."
– Elbert Hubbard

50 times, the manuscript of my first book was rejected by Amazon KDP.

I have thrown my hands in the air out of disgust.

"What am I worth?"

Worthless!

Indeed, all are right in casting aspersions on my ability to do anything.

<u>All knew I could not do anything in my life except myself.</u>

"Who are you to write books?"

"You cannot even keep your dresses organized."

"You always have a difference of opinions with others."

"You are the only one who has no good terms with everyone

in our housing society."
"You love to criticize everyone and every policy of national and global importance."
"Do you think you-know-all?"
To everyone, my failure was a foregone conclusion long before I could start any new venture. I undoubtedly had more failures than anybody around my known circle. I was always the focus of caustic criticism at every gathering in my absence. I was a reference point for an embodiment of failures in life. The rest were good people. They qualified all the litmus tests of our so-called social markers. Their net worth was very high.
They were the husbands with high ratings. They were the most intelligent, well-behaved, and always on the right side of masculinity, manner, etiquette, academic, and professional excellence. They were the best better halves. They were good sons, students, employees, and husbands. I was compared with their datum level. I was disqualified on every count.
Let me give a glaring example of a difference that made many people distance themselves from me for years. The Taj Mahal is one of the world's wonders. Every year, millions of tourists from all over the world visit it. It is the living epitome of a king's love for his queen. Love is immortalized on the planet by a tower. It has virtually become a love tourism hot spot. People feel that their loved ones are blessed to visit it. Exception-beholders got to be a nut only. I was that.
The Taj Mahal was commissioned in 1631 by Shah Jahan, the 5th Mughal Emperor, to house his wife's tomb. It was built in Indo-Islamic and Mughal architecture, in its entirety, in 1653 for around 32 million rupees, equal to 35 billion Rupees in 2023. Subsequently, it is also home to his tomb. UNESCO

designated it as a World Heritage site in 1983. Between the 2021-2021 and 2021-2022 periods, there was a 161.5% growth in domestic visitors to it. There was a 330.8% increase in overseas visitors here during the same period.

Along with being a renowned symbol of love, the Taj Mahal symbolizes Shah Jahan's wealth and power and the empire's prosperity under his rule [1].

Sir Edwin Arnold was an English poet and journalist best known for his work ***The Light of Asia***. Arnold describes it as ***"not a piece of architecture, as other buildings are, but the proud passion of an emperor's love wrought in living stones."***

Mumtaz was born in Arjumand Banu Begum in Agra to a family of Persian nobility. She was the daughter of Abu'l-Hasan Asaf Khan, a wealthy Persian noble who held high office in the Mughal Empire, and the niece of Empress Nur Jahan, the chief wife of Emperor Jahangir and the power behind the emperor. Shah Jehan married her when she was 19 years old in 1612. She gave birth to 14 children in their 17 years of married life. She died in 1631 during the birth of her 14th child (8 sons and six daughters, 7 of whom died at birth or a very young age). He built the Taj Mahal as a tomb for her, considered a monument of undying love. [2]

Virtually every year in their married life of 17 years, she continued to give birth to children one after another and finally died due to complexities arising out of pregnancies. She died from postpartum hemorrhage while giving birth to her 14th child after a prolonged labor of around 30 hours. Think briefly and try to visualize it in today's scenario by any standard.

Mumtaz Mahal was his second wife, but he had a third wife: Izz-un-Nissa Begum, the daughter of a prominent Mughal courtier.[2]

Opinions may differ. Everyone is entitled to have their own. However, the safest bet is to remain ignorant about yourself and the environment in which you are born, brought up, and lead your life. It is said – that ignorance is bliss.

Just fall in line. Be a so-called obedient child and comply with the beliefs chanted, perhaps millions of times, until they become your own.

No.

I was not. Nor am I today. You can use the idioms of your school days: ***"a hard nut to crack'***. Yes.

After all, a historical place on earth with the prestigious tagline ***'world wonder'*** is visited by millions every year, and the number of visitors from all over the globe is increasing phenomenally.

The simple thing for me is that the cause is equally important to the outcome. There is no problem with the structures humans built on this earth. It signifies the beliefs and determination of a race to uphold the forms of massive structures that take even hundreds of years to construct or thousands, as in the case of the Great Wall of China. It is the impeccable human rights beliefs in their lives as much as the richness of their culture and heritage. It serves as a constant reminder for the nation and serves the purpose of a lighthouse to give direction in their life. It equally displays the richness of tastes in their engineering quest for excellence, besides its inherent values. It is worth spending treasure to preserve as a monument for future generations. It is a legacy created by humanity on this planet.

However, what if it serves only the individual whim and fancy and the dominant power to execute it physically? In no way does it serve the purpose of others' aspirations.

I have also visited this mausoleum. However, before and after my visit, it never appeared in my mind as the structure that catches the imagination or aspirations of a nation. Especially when the citizens suffer cruel, untimely death due to draught for three years successively and humans eating the flesh of another human. Are you a beast? It was a historical landmark that existed simultaneously during Shah Jehan's rule when a famine known as the Deccan Famine broke out in 1630-32 in Deccan, Gujarat, and Khandeshi due to three main crop failures. Two million died of starvation, and grocers sold dogs' flesh and mixed powdered bones with flour, causing the plague, disease, and large-scale displacement. It is reported that parents ate their children. Some villages were destroyed, their streets filled with human corpses. [3] The Taj Mahal was commissioned by Shah Jehan in 1631.

However, according to British economist Angus Maddison, who specializes in qualitative macroeconomic history, including measurement and analysis of economic growth and development, Mughal-era India's share of global gross domestic product (GDP) grew from 22.7% in 1600 to 24.4% in 1700, surpassing China to become the world's largest. The country's financial prowess and military strengths were indeed available when millions were dying of starvation. Famine was further intensified by the Mughal campaign led by Shah Jehan in Malwa and Deccan after Malwa's Mughal commander turned rogue and joined hands with the Deccan forces of

Nizam Shah and Adil Shah. About three million people died in Gujrat in the ten months ending in October 1631, while another million died around Ahmednagar. The report gives the overall death toll of 7.4 million by late 1631, which might be the whole region. Carts belonging to banjara (carriers) transporting grain from more productive regions of Malwa were intercepted, and supplies were diverted to feed Shah Jehan's royal army in Burhanpur, who were fighting territorial wars in the Deccan (southern provinces. The feminine price of wheat was one mahmudi (its silver coin, 5.62gms, 14.70 mm, Mulher mint, Mahmudi coinage struck at Mulher by Rajah of Baglama in the name of Jala a—Uddin Muhammad Akbar the Great and according to the account books of the European trading companies' specific articles were accounted for in rupees, whereas others consequently in mahmudis) [4] per man; in 1631, it had risen to 16. Gujarat was one of the leading production centers for calico cloth, and this trade was severely affected by the death and migration of weavers [5].

Like many of my contemporaries, friends, and relatives, I could never accept that proposition to uphold the Taj Mahal as the epitome of love. It was and is instead a monument that failed humanity, which could have been avoided. It symbolized macabre on a disproportionate scale, let loose with impunity.

Richard Branson, Founder of Virgin Group and author of several books and multifaceted talent, has dyslexia and also has ADHD. He does not shy away from talking about it. He has had poor academic performance. On his last day at school, his headmaster, Robert Drayson, told him he would end up in prison or become a millionaire. [6]

But what about the outlook of our society toward dyslexia,

ADHD, and other neurodiverse 'not sufficient enough' categories of people in our society? We have low expectations from them. Is it not? We treat them secluded. We do not allow our 'sufficient enough' children to mingle with them. Even a separate identity is created for them in the "special education class." These classes or schools isolated them from peers both physically and academically. Over time, we make them believe that they could not excel at anything. These stereotypes take a toll on their self-esteem. They are not meant for success. If they become successful by sheer determination, still these students will be forced to confront again with poor expectations and stereotypes for people with dyslexia and ADHD. However, they still have become successful, and these stereotypes are deeply rooted, causing negative consequences of anxiety and depression.

Branson wanted to understand the unique value of people with dyslexia, and he wanted society to understand that dyslexia is just a different way of seeing the world. It is a different way of processing information and an opportunity to develop great ideas. To bring this message across, he started working with ***Made by Dyslexia*** [7] many years ago, proving it to be a very impactful partnership. He even worked with LinkedIn to change the Dictionary.com definition of 'dyslexia,' encouraged LinkedIn to add '***Dyslexic Thinking***' to its list of recognized skills, delved into the aggregated power of dyslexia and AI, and much more.[8]

1.2 Your Understanding: Your Discretion

"The eye sees only what the mind is prepared to comprehend."
– Robertson Davies

Each of us holds a unique lens through which we perceive the world. Just as the sun rises in one place, it sets in another. This is the beauty of our individuality and the power of our perception.

Maybe while one sees A. half an empty glass, you may see B. half full, and another may see C. both half empty and half full or D. half full and half filled with air.

Is there any way that everyone can say what the unique status of the glass is? It will not. It is purely subjective. Say you had your understanding A. With this understanding at first sight, you moved on in your life. What are the probable outcomes you may visualize?

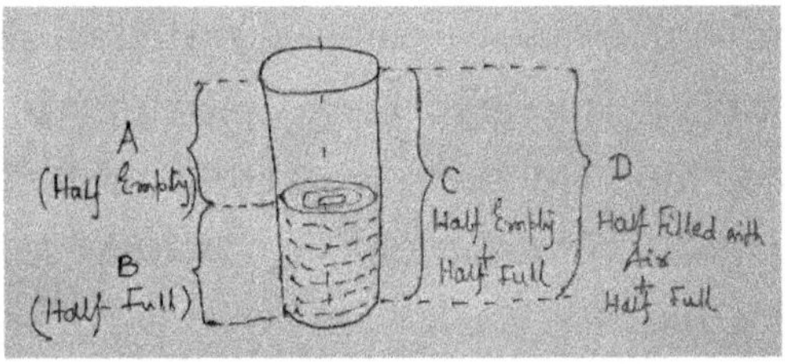

(Picture credit Author) Figure 1.1

Your focus is only on the water in the glass. There is nothing wrong with that, as that is what you can see now. Your eyes only played their role. When you drink the water, you feel insufficient to quench your thirst. Your attention will be drawn by the emptiness of the glass by half, and with half glass, more water can be accommodated. So, at that point, you realized it was half empty. Before that moment, that half-empty failed to draw your attention. It is what you learned as an outcome of your initial understanding. So, with this light of experience, you picked up a valuable lesson that will enable you to view anything in the future from a broader angle rather than a conscious observation—a lesson of life worth learning.

5 Similarly, when you see the glass as half empty, your attention is drawn to the empty portion. You fail to notice that there is still half a glass of water. When you are not thirsty, you ignore the half glass of water. What happens when your two friends come and ask for water, and you take cognizance of existing water? However, you also felt it was not sufficient. So, in this case, your initial understanding got self-scrutinized and stood self-corrected, too.

You are conscious of its entire content when you perceive the glass as half empty and complete. This flexibility in perception allows you to understand and consider various viewpoints, a valuable skill in navigating real-life situations.

7 As your understanding draws closer to the glass, your other perception could be that it is not half empty but rather half full of air. You are right. You could visualize that it is not half empty or vacuumed but half full of air. Here, your visualization is more accurate than half-empty alone. It is a qualitative assessment.

Your perspective, no matter what it is, is crucial. The key is that you have the autonomy to use your mind and decision-making abilities independently, free from external influence. This process of self-reflection and independent thinking is a powerful tool for personal growth and self-awareness.

1.3 Exercise Your Right to Make Mistakes: High ROI

"Mistakes are the portals of discovery."
– James Joyce

Accept the fact that you have the right to make mistakes. It is acceptable. After all, it is not you alone, but none is perfect. Instead, when you start complying with the opinions of others, you lose the precious opportunity to learn a valuable life lesson. Moreover, what is the guarantee that that person is right?

Challenge yourself, not others. It is not your job, and you are not an expert in others' lives. Your sincere effort should be to take risks and decide independently. If things go wrong, take ownership of the situation. You can correct it based on your understanding and how you update it as needed. Over time, you will gain more valuable insights from your experiences rather than relying on others' advice, which may or may not be suitable. Take accountability for your decisions. Do not blame others. This will free you from the fear or shame of others' judgment.

It takes some time to learn and develop the capacity for broader consideration. However, it is a quality that has the potential to unleash your capability to think independently, even if it goes wrong. Some time is wasted; instead, go with what others say, be it your friends, colleagues, or relatives. They cannot envision your imagination and the way you make decisions. Thus, time is seemingly wasted as your understanding is less mindful. Still, it certainly will save you time in the future when navigating any situations or problems with a multiplier effect. Because you are less likely to make any error in understanding, you will be able to gain a better understanding. Time is the only precious resource that can never be recovered once wasted. In this process, you earned the time defacto. ROI (Return on Investment) is exponentially higher.

1.4 Your Beliefs: Fundamentally Dysfunctional

"A belief is not merely an idea the mind possesses; it is an idea that possesses the mind."

– Robert Oxton Bolt

What if the negative perceptions of people around you finally could decapitate your ability to fight your challenges of being ADHD? Maybe it could become as overwhelming for your parents as it is for you. You can underestimate yourself. After all, our society is not broad-minded enough to encourage others. We are preoccupied with our well-being only. There is no room for others, or more specifically, for others' well-being, and that too if it happens to be for someone with dyslexia or ADHD.

Others' behavior reflects their attitude towards these insufficiencies. Their attitude is modulated accordingly because they are afraid to face such challenging situations. They are not at all able to think of something better or more constructive. The parents must first handle the problematic situations arising from such neurodiversity before a child experiences them.

Because they are tedious and lack clarity or certainty, this does not mean we should avoid such unpleasant situations. We have the self-generated feeling about "not sufficient enough." Nevertheless, when Richard Branson struggles and proves himself, the world does not notice. However, that does not mean every parent or child will be as enthusiastic about handling challenges like dyslexia or ADHD.

So, those negative beliefs of others are "not sufficient enough" and are based on an untested charter of life's journey. Just because you are incapable does not give you the authority to judge others and their abilities. Branson even went much beyond to establish the winning factors of those children having dyslexia or ADHD by showcasing to the world their unique abilities to act and think differently.

People often try to superimpose others' activities based on their poor experiences, knowledge, or untested beliefs prevailing in our society. These dysfunctional beliefs are powerful enough to make you feel "you are not enough." It is an avoidable crime against humanity. People often become wise to advise others in their hour of crisis or misery. It needs to be stopped. If you cannot support others in crisis, do not push them to the brink.

1.5 Your judgments: Your prerogative

"When you judge another,
you do not define them;
you define yourself."
-Wayne Dyer

What if my decisions go wrong?
What if I fail to prove it?
What if I am ostracized in my community?
What if I go against my elders?
Am I sufficient enough?
These are the general considerations that overshadow our capacity to make independent decisions. Let me say that you are entitled to think so for the moment.
Hay! Look here for the facts.
Somewhere, 55 countries in the world retain the practice of the death penalty.
For every eight people executed in the US, one person has been innocent, an unacceptable margin of error. "Ten guilty persons should escape than that one innocent suffers," quoted William Blackstone, an English jurist who authored commentaries on the laws of England. He lived in England from 1723 to 1780. English settlers in the American colonies took his legal

theories and used them as the basis for the American legal system.[9]

Why do we kill people who kill people to show people that killing people is wrong?

Some claim the death penalty deters crime, yet nothing could be further from the truth – and study after study refutes this.

One of the most frustrating aspects of the death penalty is the well-documented risk of executing innocent people.

Notwithstanding the outcome, more than 250 notable leaders, including Sheryl Sandberg, Alan Jope, Marc Benioff, and Richard Branson, called for an end to capital punishment worldwide. We do not always succeed, but their work is hoped to help people and governments understand why it is time to end the death penalty for good.[8]

So, if you take an opinion based on this knowledge and understanding that the death penalty should go. You are not wrong. It may not be agreeable to many. So, what? You are not bound to belong to any herd community.

What is wrong when I consider the diametrically opposite actions Shah Jehan took in commissioning the Taj Mahal as an epitome of love contrary to the truth? It was a barbaric act to be inhuman to fulfill lust and, after that, use a beautiful wrapper to glorify the act. That was also at a phenomenal cost when millions of people were dying out of sheer starvation and started behaving worse than the animals. In the name of tokenism of "langar," the grain carts were diverted to feed the soldiers who were virtually trying to grab the sovereignty of another country forcefully.

I remained an outcast. So, how does it matter to me? Nothing, even though millions visit it. Most people may not even be aware of the historical fact of cruelty perpetrated by the most influential person in this part of the world at that time. It is indispensable to understand that you are within your right to take a knowledgeable view, although you may not be on the so-called right side of the mass tribe.

Remember, the strongest person is one who stands alone. Only the creepers need support.

1.6 10 Main Takeaways from Chapter 1: Unconventional Wisdom: Embrace Your Truth

1. **Embrace Failure as a Learning Tool:** The story of the Taj Mahal and Richard Branson highlights how failure can be a stepping stone to success. The author faced 50 manuscript rejections, while Branson struggled with dyslexia and ADHD, demonstrating that repeated failures can lead to eventual success.
2. **Challenge Conventional Wisdom:** The Taj Mahal, often seen as a love symbol, can also be viewed as a monument of misplaced priorities during famine. Questioning accepted narratives can lead to deeper understanding and personal growth.
3. **Understand Your Unique Perspective:** Personal perspectives are subjective and valuable, like views on a half-full or half-empty glass. Recognizing and valuing your unique viewpoint helps you navigate life holistically.

4. **Right to Make Mistakes:** Accepting and learning from mistakes is crucial. Making independent decisions and owning outcomes fosters growth more effectively than following others' advice, which may not suit your unique situation.
5. **Self-Belief Over Social Expectations**: Society imposes limiting beliefs, especially on those with ADHD or dyslexia. Overcoming negative perceptions and believing in your potential is essential for personal success.
6. **Critique of Social Judgments**: Negative judgments faced by individuals with learning differences highlight the need for a more inclusive society. Emphasizing neurodiverse strengths fosters compassion and understanding.
7. **Impact of Historical Actions on Present Perceptions:** The Taj Mahal's construction during a famine shows how past actions shape current perceptions. Understanding this context forms nuanced opinions about historical symbols.
8. **Value of Independent Thinking**: Independent thinking is crucial for personal growth. Developing the courage to think and act independently leads to authentic and fulfilling life choices.
9. **Redefining Success and Worth:** Success should be measured by personal growth and learning, not societal benchmarks. The author's and Branson's experiences show that perceived failures can lead to significant achievements and self-discovery.
10. **Power of Vulnerability:** Embracing vulnerability is a powerful tool for personal development. Confronting

weaknesses and fears builds resilience and self-understanding, leading to a more authentic and empowered life.

Chapter 2: Shifting Perspectives: Understanding the Power of Mindset

On April 17, 2024, Day 2 of **TED 2024** was a whirlwind of new ideas as attendees joined them for the first full day of talks, ***Discovery Sessions*** (Expert-led experiences), and interactive exhibits. The process of deliberation for 2024 is named ***Spark***.

TED's mission is to discover and champion the ideas shaping tomorrow. Powerful ideas, powerfully presented, can move us to feel something, to think differently, to take action, and to create a brighter future.[10]

TED finds these powerful ideas across disciplines and around the globe from people who passionately seek a deeper understanding of the world and want to make a difference in it. TED's spotlight and its engaged, open-minded audience help these ideas create real impact: to shift one person's perspective, to make a difference within a community, or to spark global transformation.

'Ideas change everything.' [11]

On the second day's event, here are four tips they want to share with you to help you fuel your learning journey — no matter where you are:

1. Allow time for chance with an open stance

"We are boxed into believing that the world is dangerous, so it takes bravery to push yourself," says serial entrepreneur **Ramana Rao** [12]. "You have to allow time for change and take an open stance. Put yourself in environments where people travel somewhere new, reading what they have never read, learning what they did not already know." That keeps him returning to TED repeatedly — 24 times, to be exact!

2. Make vulnerability a daily practice

"To be curious, you have to jump out of a safe place," says TED speaker and mental health advocate Gus Worland [13]. "You have good days, bad days, and other points throughout a single day – but you must be willing to be vulnerable."

Gus says he lived in a safe bubble and never questioned the world he grew up in for most of his life. Then, at 48, he found himself having conversations with more and more people outside of that bubble, and he made an important discovery: he was not being curious enough.

Being vulnerable has helped Gus break out of that safe bubble. It also made him more emotional, giving him some of his life's best (as well as some of the saddest) times — which he also reflects on in his compelling talk.

3. Find ways to cultivate resilience

"When we are in our comfort zones, we are not growing," says **Nidhi Tewari** [14]. "But when we can push ourselves on an emotional, mental, spiritual, physical level to expand beyond our comfort zone – that is where we cultivate resilience."

Developing resilience has helped Nidhi adapt and bounce back from adversity, challenges, and setbacks.

4. Know yourself — but lead with curiosity

"One of the most important things that TED reinforces is to know your mind," says civic evangelist TED2019 speaker Eric Liu [15]. "Instead of assuming you know something or resting on long-held beliefs, be willing to be curious about the world around you – about politics, religion, science, work, and every aspect of life." The TED community kindles my curiosity: How did I believe this? Moreover, why do I see the world this way? After that, TED writes in the post: What is your advice for getting a new perspective?

My only advice: Embrace Vulnerability.

As long as you remain in the cocoon of dysfunctional beliefs, you are in your comfort zone.

You live like a moving cabbage only.

You are on 'autopilot ' mode.

You will always remain Lilliput of Gulliver Travel.

You wait for retirement when you join a job and wait 'as if' for death after retirement.

Such nonsensical issues will be the byproduct.

You will dance lifelong to others' choreography only.

Is this life worth it?

NO.

Under a circumstance, you realize a tectonic shift in your status quo: you acted as a clown to cheer others.

The crowd vanished, searching for new shows, and you remain in the gutter of life. Moreover, that is what you have to make yourself worth. People will desert you. Your stakeholders will refuse you to recognize and forget about their appreciation.

It is only then that you gasp for life. It would be best if you embraced Vulnerability by displaying your weakness, fear, shame, inner unhappiness, and agonizing untold pain inflicted by one and all.

You must display your eagerness to seek support to stand erect and learn to live the life of your dreams.

It is when you can develop a new perspective- authenticity.

Resilience in you does exist, and now it will show its magic.
Following is **John Fullbright's** response to that post.
Writes John Fullbright [17] Getting out of our comfort zones! In 2004, When I was struck by lightning, my body began rejecting life and me at the same time. I lost 60 lbs. from the internal burns, yet I also realized "A hole" had blown through my "hardened beliefs." Ten years of recovery later, I found a cause for a new level of disability I was experiencing-Neurological Lyme Disease. Now, after ten years, I am once again an athlete, Swiftwater Search and Rescue Technician, Researcher, and Practitioner of Ancient Tao Medicine and Japanese.
Hoshindo Meridian Apitherapy. If not for the struggles to regain my life, I would not have opened my mind far enough to have imagined what I would be doing today! Life is unbelievably good again!
The image below is entitled, "Not my last photo," taken two weeks before my being hit by lightning in Bridger Bowl, Montana, on a "Vision Quest"[16]

John (John the Lightning Bee Guy) Fullbright is now a Disaster Response Consultant, Consulting, Lightning and Lyme Disease Speaker, Bee Venom Expert, Certified Health Coach, Tao Med Astrology, Japanese Hoshindo Meridian Apitherapy and Amp Pu Ku (Organ Acupressure), Breathwork from Taos, New Mexico, United States writes

me:

Steven Covey was his earliest mentor in 1989.

I am working on my book and have written a couple of movie concepts. I am working on validating bee venom acupuncture as a traditional medicine that should be made available worldwide for long-term COVID-19 and many neurological issues like Lyme, Parkinson's, and ALZ, etc.... I am on a mission

to help people. I love India, too! I used to guide there in Zanskar and Ladakh, Manali, Rishikesh, etc....

How lightning brought out dormant Lyme Disease and pushed me into trying bee venom acupuncture, so I am now a worldwide expert on using acupuncture with bee venom for treating neurological conditions like TBI or other nerve issues...

It is also an introduction to how five-element therapy like acupuncture works...

It is nice to make friends.

My only answers were:

Amazing indeed.

You are doing a great job.

You are a valuable person full of great insights.

I consider myself fortunate to contact you.

He assured me: Thank you.

Happy to keep you posted!

Yes. John Fullbright is my hero. He is the man in the arena.

2.1 The Impact of Mindset on Success

"Whether you think you can or cannot – you are right."
-Henry Ford

Do you agree with his quote?
To understand what determines your success, let me clarify outright: It is not your talent, intelligence, or education. Maybe you also believe that it is all about suitable opportunities.
Various research suggests that your mindset is the key.
After publishing my response on TED2024, categorically advocating to Embrace Vulnerability, many responded, and more messaged me through DMs. I will share only one story, one of which is that of Mr. Raju from India.
Victim of false parenting arising out of the detrimental perception of modern success.
He is still working in the USA's IT sector, drawing a salary of Rs. 5 Cr per year. He graduated from one of the IITs, a premier League academy institution for engineering undergraduates in India. When he contacted me, he was undergoing severe depression, stopped going to the office, and was somehow struggling to retain his job. He was on the verge of resigning. In the USA, he lives alone and has been married for seven years without any children. On his last visit, his parents found him totally shattered personality, and apparently, there was no dispute in his married life. His parents became anxious and

took him to a temple nearby. It seems nothing worked. Seeing his constantly debilitating condition, his old parents, too, got sick. *Finally, Raju decided to do two things: resign from his job and divorce his wife.*

His desperate bid to Save his (our) Soul (SOS).

At this crucial juncture, he DMed me. Seeing the urgency, I stopped writing this book and instead agreed to listen to him. It took him almost one hour and forty-five minutes to speak nonstop until he became silent. I just heard him attentively one way, except for a few brief queries for clarity. I broke the silence after two minutes and asked, " Dear, how are you feeling now?" He breathed a deep sigh and said this was the first time he could share his untold inner suffering that had agonized him for seven years entirely inside out. He felt relieved.

What was his authentic problem?

After his marriage, he could never express his physical desire to his wife for seven long years.

Sounds incredible?

Is it?

I strongly suggest you pause and reflect as you read it.

His entire childhood was designed, controlled, and strictly monitored by his parents, who had a single dream: to make him study in IITs only. He was never allowed to play or mingle with his classmates. He was made to hop constantly from one class to another until he qualified to study at IIT. In IIT, another race started to make him the best product for the highly competitive job market.

How did lack of conversion devastate his life?

He never learned how to communicate with his friends and

peers and never faced academic failure. *He never encountered failure until he entered the job market in the competitive corporate world, where toxicity played havoc.* These days, the greater the corporate competition, the greater the frequency of meeting failures. That is how challenges are defined and your capacity to face them repeatedly till you succeed.

He suffered most inhumanly for none of his faults.

A problem that seemed frivolous to many took its toll before my eyes. It took him a week or so to explore the idea of communication until he gained enough self-confidence. Two days ago, he conveyed that he was neither resigning nor divorcing his wife. The magical power of communication was at foray, but he suffered so much for none of his faults.

***The only solution is to* "Fail More- Fail Fast."** [18]

One can become resilient only in the face of failure, as that is the only way to succeed and grow. I love to say, 'Fail More – Fail Fast.'

Ultimately, the difference did not lie in abilities but in minds and beliefs. In her book ***Mindset: The New Psychology of Success: The Fixed and Growth Mindsets*, Carol S. Dweck**, ***a researcher with a Ph. D. in development psychology***, identified two concepts determining people's development and success.

Fixed mindset: People with a fixed mindset believe, either consciously or unconsciously, that intelligence is unchanging. They believe that you are born with a certain degree of intellect and that your talents and qualities are stable and impossible to change. This mindset leads to particular behaviors:

1. Constantly trying to prove themselves and seem intelligent and qualified.

2. Avoid challenges at all costs because failure would mean they are incapable.
3. Getting defensive when obstacles appear and quickly giving up on challenging tasks.
4. Believing that making an effort is useless and that failure is unacceptable. They are perfectionists.
5. Finding other people's success and constructive criticism threatening.

Growth Mindset: On the other hand, people with a growth mindset believe that, with hard work and effort, you can develop your talents and abilities. Although they understand that everyone has to start somewhere, they believe what matters is what you do with what you have. This mentality leads to the following behaviors:

1. Feeling enthusiastic about learning, growing, and broadening their horizons.
2. Accepting challenges and growing with them. They consider obstacles to improvement opportunities.
3. Considering failure part of their journey. Far from letting obstacles get in their way, they persevere.
4. Considering effort as the only path to mastery instead of evidence of a lack of ability.
5. Learning from constructive criticism and being inspired by other people's success.

Reach your maximum potential:

Your mindset and the attitudes that stem from that mindset determine what you will be able to achieve. People with a fixed mindset believe their qualities are innate and unchanging, meaning they do not strive to improve. On the other hand, according to **Dweck's Theory**, people with a growth mindset who focus on effort and perseverance will continue to grow until they reach their potential. [19]

2.2 Breaking Free from Limiting Beliefs

"Do not let the noise of others' opinions drown out your inner voice."
– Steve Jobs

John Fullbright remained paralyzed in his bed for a decade after being stuck by the lightning. He could have spent his whole life at the mercy of others. There are many as of now. However, he vehemently refused to be on the receiving end as a burden for himself and others. He defied the general belief systems of so-called destiny. He declared war against this sickening belief system. He took charge of his life instead.

Being a homosapien, your brain is the most superior on this planet. You are bound to dream. Your dreams either propel you forward or hold you back in life. What limits the boundary of your dreams? It is nothing but your beliefs about yourself that limit you. In the heart of every dreamer, silent whispers of doubt in your mind tell you:

You cannot.

You are not worthy.

It is impossible.

These are the self-limiting beliefs. It holds you back in your life like an octopus.

You are born from past experiences, societal messages, and

internalized fears, and these beliefs shape your reality. Your journey to personal freedom begins with recognizing these invisible chains.

I welcome you to explore these curses that incapacitate you to foster and flourish. This is a call to action for anyone ready to challenge the narratives limiting your greatness to a lump of flesh and blood. Defy it. It is your life. You have only one life. Let your voice prevail supreme.

We delve deep into unraveling the complex web of self-imposed barriers, offering a beacon of hope and practical strategies for those who seek to redefine their lives. Through self-discovery, mindfulness, and actionable steps, you will learn how to dismantle and overcome the limiting beliefs holding you back and pave the way for a life filled with possibilities, success, and genuine personal fulfillment.

Embarking on this path is not for the faint of heart—it requires courage, introspection, and a steadfast commitment to growth. However, the rewards of such a journey are immeasurable. By confronting and overcoming your limiting beliefs, you unlock the door to a world where your dreams are not just possibilities but inevitable realities.

Look at John Fullbright or Raju as a lighthouse who is very much triumphant in this journey and standing tall on this earth to begin this transformative journey together, armed with the knowledge and tools to break free from the chains of limitation and step into the light of unbounded potential.

What are Limiting Beliefs:

At the core of our journey to personal liberation lies a critical step: understanding limiting beliefs, their origins, and their profound impact on our lives. This understanding involves identifying these beliefs and recognizing their power over our decisions, behaviors, and, ultimately, our destiny.

Definition and Examples of Common Limiting Beliefs

Limiting beliefs are deeply held convictions that constrain you in some way. Convincing us of our limitations prevents us from pursuing opportunities, taking risks, or believing in our capacities. Common examples include beliefs like:

"I am not good enough."

"I do not deserve success."

"Change is dangerous."

These beliefs often manifest as barriers to our goals and dreams in various aspects of life, from career and relationships to personal health and well-being.

Psychological and Social Origins of Limiting Beliefs

The roots of limiting beliefs are often buried deep in your past, stemming from childhood experiences, societal messages, and cultural norms. Psychologically, they may originate from critical comments from parents, teachers, or peers that we internalize as truths about our identity and abilities. Socially, they can arise from our community's values and expectations, which may dictate what is acceptable or achievable.

Our natural aversion to discomfort and fear of the unknown further reinforces these beliefs. Our brain tends to favor familiar patterns and routines over the uncertainty and risk associated with change, even if they are unhelpful or limiting. This psychological tendency makes breaking free from limiting beliefs challenging, as it requires stepping out of our comfort zone and confronting deeply ingrained fears.

While vast humanity believed the Taj Mahal to be the living testimony of a king's love for his queen, I had reasons to believe it was opposed. I was marginalized. However, I was vindicated, as my conviction stood with solid arguments and evidence, which were nothing personal but causes of human values. I stood to be judged.

The Impact of Limiting Beliefs on Daily Life and Personal Growth

The influence of limiting beliefs extends far beyond momentary doubts or fears. They can shape our reality, dictating our choices and the opportunities we pursue or let pass by. Daily, they might manifest as procrastination, self-sabotage, or a lack of fulfillment in our personal and professional lives. In the long term, these beliefs can lead to life below our potential, marked by unfulfilled dreams and a sense of stagnation.

Limiting beliefs significantly hinder personal growth. Our capacity for learning, evolving, and embracing new experiences is stifled when we are convinced of our limitations. Instead of seeing challenges as opportunities for growth, we view them through a lens of fear and doubt. This prevents us from achieving our goals and discovering our true potential and the depth of our strength and resilience.

The following sections will explore strategies for identifying limiting beliefs and practical steps to dismantle them. *The journey ahead is one of liberation—a path towards a life defined not by limitations but by possibilities and growth.*

Identifying Your Limiting Beliefs:

Embarking on the journey to personal liberation requires a deep dive into the caverns of our minds to unearth the limiting beliefs that have taken root. Identifying these beliefs is the first step toward freedom and self-discovery. Here, we explore practical strategies for self-reflection and awareness, the importance of feedback, and distinguishing between beliefs that limit us and those that protect us.

Strategies For Self-Reflection and Awareness

1. ***Role of feedback from Trusted Friends or Mentors:***
   Sometimes, it is challenging to see the limiting beliefs that are so ingrained in our thought patterns. Trusted friends, family, or mentors can offer an outside perspective. They can help identify when we are selling ourselves short or our beliefs do not align with our actions. Choosing individuals who understand your goals and support your growth is essential. Their constructive feedback can be a valuable mirror reflecting the unseen barriers you have placed on yourself.
2. ***Signs that a belief is limiting rather than protective:***
   Not all beliefs that caution us are limiting; some are protective and based on wisdom and experience. So, how do you tell the difference? A limiting belief often feels constricting, brings about feelings of inadequacy, and is rooted in fear rather than facts. It typically leads to avoidance of growth opportunities. In contrast, a protective belief is based on genuine concern for well-being and leads to cautious, informed decision-making. It is rooted in understanding and love, not fear.

Understanding and identifying limiting beliefs are crucial steps toward personal growth and liberation. Through journaling, mindfulness, feedback from those we trust, and discerning the nature of our beliefs, we can dismantle the barriers we have erected around our potential. The inward journey is the first step toward a life with freedom, purpose, and an open heart.

3. ***The Power of Mindset Shift***
   The transformation from a life constrained by limiting beliefs to one of boundless potential and growth begins with a shift in mindset. This pivotal change in how we view ourselves and our abilities can be the key to unlocking our true potential. Here, we delve into the concepts of the growth mindset versus the fixed mindset, explore how changing perspectives can challenge our limiting beliefs, and share inspiring success stories of individuals who have triumphed over their restrictive beliefs.
4. **J.K. Rowling:** Before becoming one of the world's most successful authors, Rowling faced rejection from twelve publishing houses. Her perseverance, rooted in a growth mindset, led her to continue pursuing her passion for writing despite these setbacks. Her story exemplifies how believing in the potential for growth and success, despite initial failure, can lead to unimaginable achievements.

How Changing Perspectives Can Challenge Limiting Beliefs

Adopting a growth mindset is essentially about changing perspectives. It involves recognizing that the only barriers to our potential are the ones we place on ourselves. When we shift our perspective from seeing obstacles as limitations to viewing them as stepping stones, we dismantle the power of limiting beliefs. This shift encourages us to ask, "What can I learn from this?" rather than "Why can't I do this?" By fostering a sense of curiosity and resilience, we can transform our approach to challenges and setbacks, seeing them as valuable lessons rather than confirmations of our inadequacies.[21]

2.3 Harnessing the Power of Visualization and Affirmations

"When you visualize for the joy of visualizing rather than to correct some deficiency, your thoughts are purer and therefore more powerful."
-Abraham Hicks

Try to create mental images of the anticipated outcome if:
You have to face an interview for a job.
You have to appear for an examination.
Your organization will do your yearly review.
The annual results of your school are going to be announced.
You are going to date for the first time in your life.
A medical procedure is scheduled to be held on you.
Your interview will be held for Visa clearance.
You will feel instantaneous euphoria. Maybe you studied hard

and performed well in the selection test to qualify for the interview. It is a moment of celebration. Gradually, the jubilation wanes, and the fear of appearing for an interview starts seeping into your mind.

It is fear of the unknown. You are not sure about your performance in the interview. You also recalled the high standard of the organization in every KPI (key performance index), which made you proud and happy to apply for the job and qualify for the following selection round.

What exactly happened in your mind at that time?

With the very thought of facing an interview in your mind, an uneasy situation may emerge depending upon the following factors:

1. You had an experience of failure in the past;
2. You never failed in any examination in the past or
3. You remembered your friend's experience of failure.

Under the circumstances, your likely experiences would be:

1. Your throat may get dry,
2. You may feel difficulty in breathing,
3. Feeling erratic bowel movements,
4. Your sleep may get disturbed,
5. Not able to plan and focus appropriately for the interview.

Understanding Visualization

Therefore, visualization is like crafting a movie in your mind, complete with colors, sounds, and emotions. When you visualize, your brain does not distinguish between real and imagined, allowing you to program your subconscious mind with positive images and beliefs. This process stimulates your brain to recognize opportunities and take inspired actions towards your goals.

The Power of Intention

Intention acts as the guiding force behind visualization. It is the conscious decision to focus your energy on a specific desire or outcome. When you set a clear and positive intention, you align your thoughts, emotions, and actions with your desired goal. Intention is the catalyst that ignites the manifestation process, turning your thoughts into reality.

Benefits of Visualization and Intention

By embracing visualization and intention, you can experience a multitude of benefits. First and foremost, these practices enhance your focus and motivation. When you consistently visualize your goals, you are more likely to stay committed to the path that leads to success. Additionally, visualization and intention can help reduce stress and anxiety by shifting focus from worry to positive possibilities.

Techniques for Effective Visualization

Create a vivid mental image of your desired outcome to make your visualizations more impactful. See yourself achieving your goal in great detail. Add emotions and senses to your visualization to make it more immersive. Feel the joy, excitement, and fulfillment as if it is happening now. Engaging all your senses amplifies the power of your visualizations and strengthens their manifestation potential.

Incorporating Affirmations

Affirmations are positive statements that reinforce your intentions. They can help you overwrite limiting beliefs and replace them with empowering thoughts. Craft personalized affirmations that align with your goals and resonate with you deeply. Repeat these affirmations daily to create a positive and supportive internal dialogue.

Manifesting Your Goals with Visualization and Intention

Visualization and intention work hand in hand with action. While visualizing is powerful, taking practical steps toward your goals is equally essential. Align your actions with your intentions, and be open to opportunities that come your way. *Remember, manifestation is a process that requires patience and trust in the universe's timing.*

Embracing Visualization and Intention as a Daily Practice

To maximize visualization and intention, make it part of your daily routine. Find a time that works best for you, whether in the morning, during lunch breaks, or before bedtime. Create a peaceful and inspiring environment to focus on your practice without distractions. Approach it with joy and excitement, as if you embark on an enchanting adventure of creating your dream life.

Visualization and intention are powerful tools that can transform your life. By harnessing the magic of visualization, you can program your subconscious mind for success and amplify your manifestation potential. When combined to create positive change, these practices pave the way for achieving your goals, reducing stress, and manifesting abundance and fulfillment. Embrace the power of visualization and intention, and watch as your dreams become a vibrant reality.

It is a reminder that the stories you choose to engage with can shape your personal growth and the world around you.[22]

Visualization Techniques to Manifest Your Dreams:

You can achieve any goal – and create any future – you can

imagine.

However, the key to unlocking this ability rests in your ability to imagine your goals clearly and visualize the process and results of achieving them!

What is Visualization?

Let us begin with a quick overview of what positive visualization is and what an effective visualization practice looks like.

Visualization is what you do when you close your eyes and create positive mental imagery that reflects what you expect your life to look like once a particular outcome has been achieved. Do you know when you are daydreaming or imagining something and the mental images come across so clearly in your mind that it almost feels like you are there? That is what creative visualization looks like. It activates your subconscious mind to proactively seek out opportunities to accomplish the goals you have visualized yourself achieving.

Let us explore the two main visualization techniques to help you manifest your dreams.

Two different types of visualization techniques are available, each with its strengths.

Outcome visualization: This visualization technique focuses on what your life will look like once your desired outcome has been attained. You imagine as many details as possible about what this future is like for you—your days, where you live and who you spend time with, and how you feel in your body and mind as you contemplate your life in this ideal future. Outcome visualization is the carrot that pulls you forward and keeps you motivated and inspired as you work toward your goal.

Process visualization: This technique focuses on the steps to reach that desired outcome. It reduces anxiety and eliminates negative thought impulses that arise from a lack of experience or self-esteem. When you actively visualize yourself doing the research, training, building your support network, and taking the leap into unknown territory, you make it much easier to do these things. Studies show that engaging in such visualization exercises makes you far more likely to achieve better outcomes.

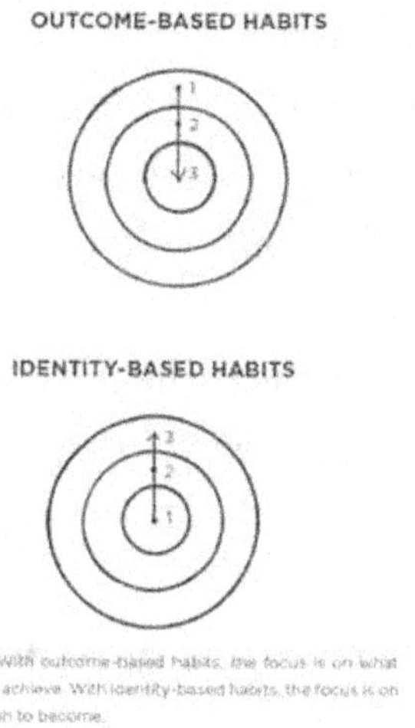

Figure 2.3.1[23]

I recommend using creative visualization techniques to strengthen your mental image and motivation.

Benefits of Visualizations:

Here is a quick overview of the specific benefits you will experience using these visualization techniques daily:

1. Visualization activates your creative subconscious,

generating creative ideas to achieve your goal.

2. It programs your brain to more readily perceive and recognize the resources you need to achieve your dreams.

3. It activates the **Law of Attraction**, thereby drawing into your life the people, resources, and circumstances you will need to achieve your goals. (More on that below.)

4. It builds your internal motivation to take the necessary actions to achieve your dreams.

5. It increases your confidence as you become increasingly able to visualize yourself as the kind of person who is capable of accomplishing your goals.

6. It helps you mitigate stress and reduce anxiety by making it easier to anticipate possible roadblocks and imagine workable solutions that will help you overcome them faster or avoid them altogether.

7. It sets you up for success by helping you "practice" success in your mind and learn to see yourself as someone who takes risks and achieves successful outcomes.

8 Visualization Techniques to Reach Your Dreams:

Use the following techniques to create effective visualization practice and move closer to achieving your life goals.

1. Know What You Want

Your first step is to pick one specific dream or goal you want to focus on and clarify what it is and why you want to achieve it. The more clearly you can define this dream or goal, the easier it will be to visualize yourself achieving it.

2. The 'Mental Rehearsal' Technique

This is one of the visualization techniques that are popular with top athletes. To practice, set aside a few minutes a day when you are relaxed, such as when you first wake up, after meditation or prayer, or right before you go to bed. Then, go through these three steps:

STEP 1. Imagine sitting in a movie theater. The lights dim, and the movie starts. It is a movie of YOU doing perfectly whatever you want to do better. Visualize what is happening on the screen in as much detail as possible – including your clothing, the expression on your face, your environment, and any other people that might be around. Add in any sounds you hear — traffic, music, other people talking, clapping. Finally, recreate in your body any feelings you think you would be experiencing as you engage in this activity.

STEP 2. Get out of your chair, walk up to the movie screen, open a door in the screen, and walk through it into the actual movie. Now experience the entire scene again from inside yourself, looking out through your eyes. This is called an ***"embodied image"*** rather than a ***"distant image"*** and will deepen the impact of the experience. Again, see, hear, and see everything in vivid detail.

STEP 3. Walk back out of the screen and return to your seat in the theater – then grab the screen where the movie of your life is still playing and shrink it down to the size of a cracker. Now eat it! Pop that tiny screen into your mouth, chew it up, and swallow it. Imagine that each tiny piece contains the complete picture of you performing well, just like a hologram. Visualize all these little screens traveling down into your stomach and through the bloodstream into every cell of your body. Then imagine that every cell of your body is lit up with a movie of you performing perfectly.

This whole process should take about five minutes. When you have finished, you can open your eyes and go about your business. If you make this part of your daily routine, you will be amazed at how much improvement you will see in your life!

3. Create a Vision Board

One of my favorite visualization techniques is using a vision board to help you visualize your goals as having been achieved. A vision board is a collage of images and powerful words or phrases that evoke the visuals, objects, and sensations you associate with achieving your goal.

For example, if one of your dreams is to own a new car, take your camera to your local auto dealer and take a picture of yourself sitting behind the wheel of your dream car. If your goal is to visit Paris, find a picture or poster of the Eiffel Tower and place a picture of yourself and the image of Paris on your vision board.

4. Write on Index Cards or Notecards

Another way to use physical aids as part of your visualization process is to write your goals on 3×5 index cards and keep those cards near your bed so you can read them out loud every morning when you first wake up and at night before you go to bed. As you read each goal out loud, see the completion of that goal in its perfect desired state for about 15 seconds, then open your eyes and repeat the process with the next card.

5. Use Affirmations to Support Your Visualization

An affirmation is a positive statement written in the affirmative present tense that evokes the experience of already having whatever you want.

Here is an example of an affirmation: "I am happily vacationing two months out of the year in a tropical paradise and working just four days a week owning my own business." Repeating an affirmation several times daily keeps you focused on your goal, strengthens your motivation, and programs your subconscious to do whatever it takes to achieve that goal. Please note that the affirmation is always focused on what you DO want to achieve, not what you DO not want to experience. This is because we always get what we visualize, even when expressed as unfavorable. (Try to consciously NOT think about pink elephants, and you will see what I mean.)

6. Create Triggers for Your Subconscious Mind

Our subconscious minds have evolved to become incredibly good at connecting sensations and experiences. That is why a particular smell can immediately evoke a powerful memory and a surge of associated emotions.

To create positive triggers for your subconscious, expose yourself to a specific sensory input as you do your visualization exercises. For example, you might want to listen to a specific song or use aromatherapy to connect a specific scent to visualize your desired outcome. Then, make sure you are exposed to that scent or song at least once a day so that your visualization springs clearly to mind.

7. Activate the Law of Attraction and Reach Your Goals

This is one of the visualization techniques I love best. The more intensely we can visualize something as complete, the more hardwired our brains are to resolve the conflict between the vision we hold in our heads and our knowledge that this reality does not exist yet.

Visualization activates the creative powers of the subconscious, motivating it to work harder at creating solutions. You will also notice new motivation levels and find yourself doing things you normally would avoid, but that will take you closer to success.

8. Live in the Moment

One of the best ways to amplify the effectiveness of any visualization techniques you use is to practice being present at the moment. Daily rituals help you balance thinking about the future and living in the "***now***." Start by picking a time during which you will review your goals and visualize your success. Ideally, do this twice daily – first thing in the morning and right before bed. The process typically takes 10 minutes or less. *If you meditate, practicing your favorite visualization techniques immediately afterward is a good idea. The deepened state of relaxation meditation will heighten the impact of your practice.*

Once you have completed your visualization techniques and visualized each goal as complete, it is time to release. Let go of your goals and spend the rest of your day in the present moment. This will help you think more clearly and react effectively to whatever is happening to get better outcomes in everything you do.

Incorporate Sensory Experiences

Focusing on your bodily sensations is an easy way to become more present in the moment instantly. However, it is impossible to focus on your physical body and be mentally in the past or the future simultaneously.

Here is an example to show you what I mean: focus on your left foot. What are you feeling? Pay attention to the sensation for a minute. Then, notice what you are feeling on your right foot and spend a few moments feeling the sensation. If you were able to pay attention to your feet, congratulations. You were present.

If you find your mind drifting to the past or future throughout the day, you can use this practice or one of the more basic visualization techniques to bring yourself back to the present moment.

As the saying goes, ***"Today is a gift—that is why it is called the present."*** Practice regular visualization techniques to help you achieve your goals, but spend most of your time enjoying today's gift. You will get better outcomes if you do!

Expect Real Results

Writing down your goals, using visualization techniques, and repeating affirmations daily can help you achieve excellent results.

Visualization and affirmations allow you to change your beliefs, assumptions, and opinions about the most crucial person in your life – YOU! They allow you to harness the 18 billion brain cells in your brain and get them all working in a singular and purposeful direction.

So, instead of dwelling on skepticism or self-doubt, I encourage you to practice positive thinking and allow yourself to believe that you have the innate capacity to achieve any goal you can imagine. If you put in the time to practice at least one powerful visualization technique every day, surround yourself with positive people, read uplifting books, and listen to audio programs that flood your subconscious mind with positive, life-affirming messages, I guarantee you will be amazed at what you will accomplish!

Practice Visualization Today

Now that you know the power of using visualization techniques to help you stay motivated and focused as you work to achieve your goals, I encourage you to get started today!
A great way to amplify the impact of your visualization techniques is to incorporate Law of Attraction strategies to raise your energetic frequency and attract more of what you need into your life.[24]

2.4 Bouncing Back from Setbacks

"Our greatest glory is not in never falling,
However, in rising every time we fall."
– Confucius

Mr. Raju decided to quit his lucrative job in Silicon Valley and divorce his wife. In the meantime, what changed his decision not to resign and bring his wife back to him from India?
At that crucial juncture, he contacted me as his last bid to try something for the last time before he nails his future and fortune.
I listened to him coolly for almost two hours, except for a few questions I asked for clarification. It was clear that, mentally, he lost his battle. He will seal his fate for life within a day or so. It was a case of someone who achieved all the distinguished academic laurels and never failed any examination, meeting the disaster. He does not know how to turn around and

retrieve his past glories of success.

I do not subscribe to the idea that something may be wrong with his spouse. As revealed, this fact gradually corroborates my basic approach to this issue. Instead, my focus was only on Mr. Raju.

How can he shift his perception from a vanquished one to the victor?

The ability to bounce back from setbacks is often described as the difference between successful and unsuccessful people. Resilience has been shown to positively influence work satisfaction and engagement, as well as overall well-being, and can lower depression levels. However, resilience is not just a kind of solitary internal "grit" that allows us to bounce back.

There is even evidence that resilience can help protect us from physical illness. However, conventional thinking assumes resilience is something we find within ourselves only when tested—a kind of solitary internal "grit" that allows those of us who are vital to bounce back. However, that is not necessarily true. Research shows that resilience is not purely an individual characteristic but is also heavily enabled by strong relationships and networks.

We can nurture and build our resilience through interactions with people personally and professionally. These interactions can help us shift or push back on work demands and alter the magnitude of our challenges. They can help crystalize the meaningful purpose in what we are doing or help us see a path forward to overcome a setback – these interactions motivate us to persist. People in our support systems can provide empathy or help us laugh and bolster our resilience by shifting perspectives and reminding us that we are not alone in the fight. In short, resilience is not something we need to find deep down inside ourselves: we can become more resilient in connecting with others in our most challenging times.

However, such a network will not materialize overnight. When we talk to people who have shown exceptional resilience, it is clear that they often have cultivated and maintained authentic connections that come from many parts of their lives — not only through work but through athletic pursuits, volunteer work, civic or religious communities, book or dinner clubs, communities of parents they have met through their children, and so on. Interactions in these spheres provide critical "dimensionality," broadening their identity and "opening the aperture" on how they look at their lives. We become more (or less) resilient through our interactions with others.

Are your relationships broad and deep enough to support you when you experience setbacks? Here is an exercise to help you consider that.

Step 1: Identify your top resilience needs.

Below are eight familiar relational sources of resilience, which we noted above. Research shows that these sources are not universally or equally important to everyone. For example, some people value laughter, while others prefer empathy. In short, our resilience needs are personal and are shaped by our unique history, personality, and professional/personal context. However, collectively, the relationships we develop are a toolbox we can turn to in our most difficult times, which we can rely upon to help us navigate daily life challenges.

Using the framework below, identify the top three sources of resilience that you would most like to strengthen in your life. Make a note of those that are most important for you to work on developing.

What Are Your Top Relational Sources of Resilience?

A well-developed network of relationships can help you rebound from setbacks. Identify the spheres that are most important to you. Are you falling short in some categories?

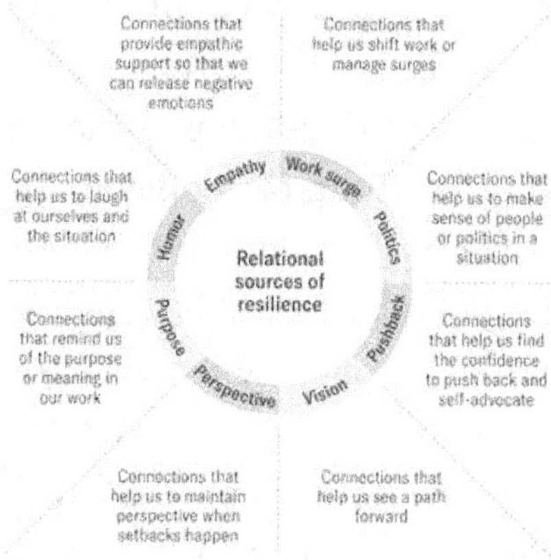

Source: Rob Cross, Karen Dillon, and Danna Greenberg © HBR

Step 2: Plan how to expand your network.

Reflecting on the top three resilience needs you indicated, place the names of people or groups you could invest in to cultivate sources of resilience further. Connections that yield resilience can be intentionally cultivated in two ways. First, we can broaden existing relationships by, for example, exploring non-work interests with a teammate or strengthening mutually beneficial relationships with influential work colleagues that help us push back. Second, we can initiate engagement with new groups or people to cultivate essential elements of resilience — for example, spiritual groups that remind us of our purpose or affinity groups that allow us to laugh. Broadening our network helps us develop dimensionality in our lives — a rich variety of relationships and connections that help us grow, that can provide perspective on our struggles, and that can offer us a stronger sense of purpose. These groups may come from any walks of life — athletic pursuits, spiritual associations, nonprofit board work, community organizing groups around social, environmental, or political issues, etc. Engaging in nonwork groups (particularly board work, social action, and community organizing groups) also helps us develop resilience in our work life. Exposure to a diverse group of people allows us to learn different ways of managing, leading, and handling crises. It helps us develop different relational skills, such as negotiating with various stakeholders. It also helps us cultivate empathy and perspective that we carry back into our work, among other benefits. In summary, meaningful investment in non-work relationships broadens the toolkit one can rely upon to manage setbacks when they arise.

One critical insight from our interviews is that relying on your network in transition matters greatly. When people told us stories of significant transitions — moves, job losses, role expansions, or family changes — they tended to separate into one of two groups. One group tended to lean into the transition and relied on existing relationships to work through the ambiguity and anxiety they were experiencing. This group also used the transition to reach out to one or two new groups, such as a working parent's group, a newcomer's group, or a work-based coaching circle. In contrast, the second group operated with a mindset that they needed to absorb the transition and close in on their circle. They felt overwhelmed and said they would lean into activities when they had time. Over 18 months, this group became a smaller version of themselves and often drifted away from the connections that had been so important to their lives.

Covid has created a significant transition for us all. The importance of building and maintaining your connections has never been more evident. For most of us, the challenges and setbacks we are experiencing at work and in life during this pandemic have been relentless. However, you are not alone in this battle. You can build resilience. Start by understanding the importance of growing, maintaining, and tapping a diverse network to help you ride out the storm.[25]

2.5 Crafting Your Mantra for Success

"Success is not the key to happiness. Happiness is the key to success. If you love what you are doing, you will be successful."
– Albert Schweitzer

After reading so far, you are well acquainted with the mantra of navigating your path toward success.

Consistency is the buzzword for success in any field of life. Once you are transparent about the process to progress, what remains to be done in practice? It will be too good to practice in a prefixed time and place. However, that is not at all a prerequisite. Wherever you can, you can continue to chant those. It could be while in the bathroom, moving from place to place, waiting for your turn at a doctor's, at the airport, or in the visitor's lobby at the hospital, or waiting for examinations or interviews to start. Just be outrageous. Never mind the inevitable criticism you will encounter as you start the process. It matters to you nothing. They are just ignorant. Be compassionate to yourself and others. That is all.

Your actions may not be proper at the beginning. I strongly advocate for ***Consistent Imperfect Actions****. All the gurus on this planet were students once. They invariably made many mistakes or committed blunders like me. You, too, will.* <u>*However, the sin is if you never try.*</u>

Therefore, include a self-care mantra in your daily life. This is bound to improve overall well-being and mindset.

Self-care mantras as a daily routine give you a jump start on making peace of mind a top priority. Harnessing the power of positive affirmations is a wellness routine worth making time for. You are in the right place if you aim to level up from past mistakes or evolve your spiritual health to pursue new things.

In our fast-paced world, it is crucial to prioritize self-care and nurture our mental and physical well-being. Self-care mantras are powerful tools that can help us combat negative thoughts, set a positive tone for our mental health, and bring good vibes to our daily lives.

Here, we will explore the transformative effects of daily mantras, delve into the importance of positive self-talk, and discover how incorporating self-care practices can enhance our overall well-being. Get ready to embrace the beauty of mantra and unlock your inner strength!

The Power of Positive Affirmations

Negative thoughts breed negative energy, but positive affirmations can counteract their influence. We can rewire our minds and create a more optimistic outlook by consciously choosing positive thoughts and beliefs. Daily mantras, such as "I am worthy of love and happiness," *"I choose to embrace a healthy lifestyle,"* or "I am deserving of success," can serve as powerful reminders of our inherent worth and potential. *Repeating these affirmations ingrains them in our subconscious, positively shaping our thoughts and actions.*

Nurturing Mental Health

Our mental health relies on us to set the tone. Just as we care for our physical health, we must prioritize our emotional and mental well-being. Self-care mantras are a simple way to nurture our minds and cultivate a healthier inner voice. They help us combat negative self-talk, especially during hard times or high-pressure situations. *By replacing self-doubt with positive self-talk, we can build resilience, boost confidence, and maintain a balanced perspective.*

Embracing Self-Care Practices

Self-care practices encompass many activities that nourish our mind, body, and soul. Incorporating self-care mantras into our routine can amplify the effectiveness of these practices. Self-care mantras can be integrated into meditation, exercise, journaling, or spending quality time with loved ones. They act as gentle reminders to prioritize our well-being. *Taking a deep breath and reciting a mantra like "I am capable of overcoming any challenge" can help us navigate difficult moments with grace and composure.*

Journal Prompts for Self-Reflection

Journaling is a powerful tool for self-reflection and introspection. It allows us to connect with our innermost thoughts and emotions. When combined with journaling, the mantra becomes an even more transformative practice. Try using journal prompts such as *"What mantra resonates with me the most and why?"* or "How can I incorporate positive self-talk into my daily life?" *These prompts encourage self-discovery and provide a space for personal growth.*

The Impact on Physical Health

Embracing your whole self is a physical, mental, emotional, and energetic journey. While self-care mantras primarily focus on nurturing our mental and emotional well-being, their positive effects also extend to physical health. *Our mind and body are interconnected, and caring for one naturally benefits the other.*

When we consistently engage in self-care practices and incorporate self-care mantras into our daily routines, we create a harmonious balance within ourselves. This balance reduces stress, promotes relaxation, and improves physical health. Research has shown that chronic stress can negatively impact our immune system, cardiovascular health, and longevity. We can enhance physical well-being by actively managing stress through self-care and positive affirmations. Self-care mantras powerfully remind us to prioritize our physical health. Phrases like "I honor my body by nourishing it with healthy choices" or "I commit to regular exercise to strengthen my body and mind" can help us make conscious decisions that support our well-being. These mantras encourage us to listen to our bodies, practice self-compassion, and engage in activities that promote vitality.

Harnessing Self-Care Mantras in High-Pressure Situations

Life often presents us with high-pressure situations, whether a demanding work deadline, an important presentation, or a challenging personal situation. During these times, self-care mantras become even more valuable in helping us maintain composure, focus, and resilience.

In moments of stress, our inner voice tends to amplify negative thoughts and self-doubt. By employing self-care mantras, we can interrupt this negative spiral and replace it with positive self-talk. For instance, repeating mantras like "I am calm and capable," "I have the strength to overcome any obstacle," or "I trust in my abilities" can instill a sense of confidence and inner strength.

Self-care mantras also serve as anchors, grounding us in the present moment. Amidst chaos and pressure, deep breathing and reciting a mantra can bring clarity and center our thoughts. It allows us to regain control over our emotions and approach the situation calmly.

Integrating Self-Care Mantras into Daily Life

Bringing self-care mantras into our daily lives does not have to be complicated or time-consuming. Simplicity is key. We can create a sustainable practice that supports our overall well-being by finding simple ways to infuse our routines with positive affirmations.

Here are some ideas to integrate self-care mantras into your daily life:

Morning Rituals

Start your day by setting an intention and reciting a self-care mantra that resonates with you. For example, "Today, I prioritize my well-being and radiate positivity."

Sticky Notes

Place sticky notes with uplifting self-care mantras in

prominent locations around your home or workspace. This will remind you of these positive affirmations throughout the day.

Mindful Breaks

Take short breaks during the day to practice deep breathing and repeat self-care mantras silently or aloud. This helps reset your mind and promotes a sense of calm.

Bedtime Reflection

Before sleep, reflect on your day and recite a self-care mantra that affirms your efforts and self-compassion. It could be as simple as "I did my best today, and I am proud of myself."

Remember, consistency is critical. The more you incorporate self-care mantras into your daily life, the more they become ingrained in your thoughts and actions.

Embracing a Holistic Approach

Self-care mantras remind us to embrace our whole selves—physical, mental, emotional, and spiritual aspects. They encourage us to cultivate a healthy and remind us to embrace our whole selves—the flawed and imperfect aspects alongside our strengths and accomplishments. They promote self-acceptance and encourage us to practice unconditional love toward ourselves. By acknowledging and appreciating our uniqueness, we can foster a healthy lifestyle that prioritizes self-care and nourishes every aspect of our being.

Mantras are invaluable tools for maintaining and enhancing our well-being. By consciously choosing positive affirmations and integrating them into our daily lives, we can transform negative thoughts into positive energy. Remember, self-care is not selfish; it is a necessary act of self-love. Embrace the power of mantras, and let them guide you towards a healthier, happier, and more fulfilling life.

How do yoga and meditation help achieve all of these goals and more?

The Effectiveness and Efficiency of Yoga and Meditation:

Yoga and meditation are powerful practices that align perfectly with the goals of self-care mantras. They offer a holistic approach to nurturing our well-being, encompassing physical, mental, and spiritual aspects of our being. Let us explore how yoga and meditation can help us achieve these goals.

Cultivating Mind-Body Connection:

Yoga combines physical postures (asanas) with breath control and meditation. Through asanas, we learn to connect our breath with movement, bringing awareness to our bodies. This fosters a deep sense of presence and cultivates a harmonious mind-body connection. Syncing our movements with our breath releases tension, enhances flexibility, and improves physical strength. The physical aspect of yoga complements the mental aspect of self-care mantras, creating a balanced approach to overall well-being.

Stress Reduction and Emotional Balance:

Yoga and meditation have been widely recognized for reducing stress and promoting emotional balance. Regular practice stimulates the parasympathetic nervous system, activating the body's relaxation response and counteracting the effects of chronic stress. This helps to lower cortisol levels, decrease anxiety, and promote a sense of calm. Combined with self-care mantras, yoga, and meditation provide powerful tools to manage negative thoughts and emotions, allowing us to respond to challenging situations more resiliently and clearly.

Heightened Self-Awareness:

Meditation, in particular, cultivates self-awareness and mindfulness. We develop a deeper understanding of ourselves by sitting in stillness and observing our thoughts and sensations without judgment. This heightened self-awareness enables us to identify negative thought patterns and replace them with positive self-talk. Self-care mantras work hand in hand with meditation, providing us with positive affirmations to repeat during our practice. Combining meditation and self-care mantras empowers us to reshape our inner dialogue, fostering a more compassionate and nurturing relationship with ourselves.

Improved Mental Focus and Clarity:

Yoga and meditation enhance mental focus and clarity. As we engage in asanas and meditative practices, we learn to direct our attention to the present moment, quieting the constant chatter of the mind. This sharpened focus spills over into our daily lives, allowing us to concentrate on tasks with greater efficiency and productivity. When combined with self-care mantras, we create a positive mental environment that supports clear thinking, decision-making, and problem-solving.

Spiritual Nourishment:

For many, yoga and meditation offer a path to spiritual growth and self-discovery. These practices encourage connecting with our inner selves and accessing a more profound sense of purpose and meaning. Through self-reflection and contemplation, we explore our values, beliefs, and the essence of our being. Self-care mantras aligned with spiritual principles, such as "I am connected to the divine energy within me" or "I embrace the journey of self-discovery," can guide us on our spiritual path and provide a sense of grounding and transcendence.

Incorporating yoga and meditation into our routine enhances the transformative effects of self-care mantras. These practices offer a holistic approach to well-being, fostering physical strength, emotional balance, self-awareness, mental clarity, and spiritual nourishment. As you embark on your self-care journey, consider integrating yoga and meditation into your daily life, allowing these powerful tools to support and amplify the positive impact of self-care mantras.[26]

2.6 10 Main Takeaways: Chapter 2: Shifting Perspectives: Understanding the Power of Mindset

1. **The Power of an Open Stance and Vulnerability:** Embracing openness and vulnerability fuels personal growth. Ramana Rao advocates stepping beyond comfort zones to embrace new experiences, fostering curiosity and learning. Gus Worland underscores vulnerability's role in breaking barriers and facilitating emotional growth and connection.
2. **Cultivating Resilience:** Nidhi Tewari emphasizes resilience through discomfort. Growth across emotional,

mental, spiritual, and physical realms builds resilience, vital for overcoming challenges and achieving enduring success.

3. **Leading with Curiosity:** Eric Liu champions curiosity-driven leadership. Questioning beliefs fosters continuous learning and openness, which is pivotal for personal and communal growth.
4. **The Impact of Mindset on Success**: Henry Ford and Carol S. Dweck state that Mindset shapes success. A growth mindset views challenges as opportunities, fostering perseverance and adaptability toward achieving goals.
5. **Breaking Free from Limiting Beliefs**: John Fullbright's tale highlights overcoming limiting beliefs. Challenging such beliefs unlocks potential, enabling remarkable personal growth and achievement.
6. **Clarify Your Goals:** Start by defining a specific goal clearly and understand why you want to achieve it. The more precise your vision, the easier it becomes to visualize success.
7. **Practice Mental Rehearsal:** Adopt athletes' 'Mental Rehearsal' technique. Imagine yourself achieving your goal in vivid detail, engaging all senses. This daily practice reinforces your commitment and enhances performance.
8. **Create a Vision Board:** Use a vision board with images and words that represent your goals achieved. This visual reminder keeps your aspirations tangible and reinforces motivation.
9. **Use Affirmations:** Use positive affirmations that affirm your goals as already achieved. This helps maintain focus,

boost confidence, and align your subconscious with your objectives.

10. **Live in the Moment:** Balance visualization with present-moment awareness. Regularly review and visualize your goals, then release them and focus on present actions. This practice enhances clarity and effectiveness in daily tasks.

Chapter 3: Self-Compassion: Cultivating Emotional Intelligence for Success

3.1: Understanding Emotions: The Heart of Emotional Intelligence

"The greatest discovery of my generation is that a human being can alter his life by altering his attitudes."
– William James

The company was Enron, and the story's two protagonists were Jeff Skilling and Kenneth Lay.
Two brilliant guys:
Let me tell you the story of two very ***"smart"*** guys: **Jeffrey and Kenneth.**
Jeffrey was born in 1953 in Pittsburg, Pennsylvania. Second of four kids, he has shown to be smarter than other youngsters since childhood. This became evident when Jeffrey was finally admitted to Southern Methodist University in Dallas, receiving a full scholarship and eventually studying business. After graduation and working with a Houston bank for a while, Jeffrey was sent to Harvard Business School, graduating in the top 5% of his class (Bio).
Kenneth was born in 1942 in Tyrone, a small town in Missouri, as an only child. He was brilliant as a child and worked his tail off delivering newspapers and mowing lawns.

Subsequently, he earned a degree in economics from the University of Missouri but was not satisfied yet; he earned a PhD in economics from the University of Houston in 1970 (Bio).

What did they have in common?

They were both brilliant and successful and wanted to make money. Their paths crossed when Kenneth hired Jeffrey as a consultant (while working at McKinsey and Co.). Kenneth's company operated in the utility industry, and it was one of the biggest and most successful corporations in the US. Kenneth was impressed by Jeffrey's performance, and eventually, he hired him as CEO of the Capital & Trade Resources of the corporation (the central division of the company). Jeffrey's career was so successful that by 1997, he was nominated CEO of the whole company. Only Kenneth retained a more assertive role within the organization. It would have been great if the story ended there, but let us see what happened next!

The story unraveled:

Kenneth and Jeffrey were brilliant individuals with MBAs, PhDs, and very high IQs; therefore, they were destined to succeed.

Jeffrey and Kenneth were not the only intelligent guys in the company. Since Jeffrey became CEO, top graduates were hired to run the company's operations. The company became so successful that Kenneth and Jeffrey were everywhere, from business magazines to finance newspapers.

Their reputation on Wall Street proliferated. How did the company grow so fast?

Jeffrey had the brilliant idea to use market-to-market accounting. This means the company values its assets at market value instead of historical cost. For example, when the company invests in new plants, although profit has not been made yet, it could already show its future estimated profits on the balance sheet. If the acquired plant did not produce any profit in the future, the company created ad hoc off-balance sheet financial vehicles to hide the losses. Therefore, the company balance sheet was always "clean" from losses. Those complex operations allowed the company to keep a high rating while not risking a dime. However, were all those operations legal? As it turned out, they were not. Indeed, when the operations became too complex, the company could not hide them anymore, and the financial situation became unbearable. When voices spread that the company had billions lost in those operations, it became one of the greatest scandals in American history. The company was ***Enron***, and the story's two protagonists were Jeff Skilling and Kenneth Lay. ***They were "the smartest guys in the room."*** [29]

In 2006, Jeff and Kenneth were convicted of fraud, which became the most evident case of how intelligent people can do stupid things.

Is it possible that **Jeffrey *and* Kenneth**, among the most intelligent people on the planet, could not foresee the risk involved in their operations? Maybe they did understand the risk rationally but not emotionally. However, can we still define those people as intelligent if that is the case?

Of course, they are among the people with the **highest IQ** in the world.

What is the other aspect of intelligence that goes beyond IQ?

Emotions. *Indeed, emotions can hijack the intelligence of an* *individual.* **Daniel Goleman** calls it ***"EI"*** or ***"Emotional Intelligence."*** Although the term ***"Emotional intelligence"*** was used for the first time by ***psychologists*** **John Mayer and Peter Salovey**, Goleman formulated a systematic approach to EI.

What is emotion?

Emotions include feeling, thought, nervous system activation, physiological changes, and behavioral changes such as facial expressions. Emotions seem to dominate many aspects of our lives as we have to recognize and respond to critical events related to survival and the maintenance of prosperity, and, therefore, emotions serve various functions.[27]

According to Darwin, all people, regardless of race or culture, express emotions similarly using their face and body as part of our evolutionary heritage. Emotion is often defined as a complex feeling that results in physical and psychological changes affecting thought and behavior. [28]

What is Emotional Intelligence (EI)?

How often have you found yourself doing something you promised would not happen again?

Examples include saying something in public you were not supposed to say or falling again into an old bad habit you were trying to abandon.

In all those cases, we fall back into the trap because we lack Emotional Intelligence, or "the capacity to assert self-control, persistence and most of all to motivate oneself." Why is it so difficult to change our bad habits or behaviors?

Try to stop and think for a few seconds about how many times you burst into anger and treat people around you badly. Then, just half an hour later, you regret what you did. Why don't we stop such behaviors in the moment they are happening?

We lack emotional intelligence, or the ability to understand what we feel at a particular moment. In other words, if you are having a dispute with your family and suddenly you are about to "lose your mind," how can you avoid that?

While you talk or listen, try to analyze your internal mental state, assess your body sensations, and get out of the dispute for half an hour if you detect some discomfort. This time will allow you to clear your mind and let the cortisol (a hormone released during stressful situations) be absorbed by the organism, making you more relaxed.

Of course, this is just one situation you may face in life, but the point is that EI requires much mindfulness and the ability to see oneself from the outside. It is almost like you are inside your head while you react to something; on the other hand, you are someone else looking at yourself from the outside! Does it sound wild? It sounds overwhelming and is not easy since much practice is required. The next natural question is: Why would I waste my time doing so when I could be studying technical staff? Let me answer... [30]

3.2 Managing Emotions Effectively: Strategies for Self-Regulation

"He who controls others may be powerful, but he who has mastered himself is mightier still."

– Lao Tzu

The term ***'Emotional Intelligence,'*** first coined by psychologists **Mayer and Salovey** (1990), refers to one's capacity to perceive, process, and regulate emotional information accurately and effectively, both within oneself and in others, and to use this information to guide one's thinking and actions and to influence those of others.

Emotional intelligence can lead us to a fulfilled and happy life by providing a framework for applying intelligence standards to emotional responses and understanding that these responses may be logically consistent or inconsistent with particular beliefs about emotion.

As the workplace evolves, so does the body of research supporting that individuals (from interns to managers) with higher EI are better equipped to work cohesively within teams, deal with change more effectively, and manage stress—thus enabling them to pursue business objectives more efficiently.

Goleman (1995) recognized five distinct categories of skills that form the critical characteristics of EI and proposed that, unlike one's intelligence quotient (IQ), these categorical skills can be learned where absent and improved upon where present.

Thus, EI, unlike its relatively fixed cousin, IQ, is a dynamic aspect of one's psyche. It includes behavioral traits that, when worked upon, can yield significant benefits, from personal happiness and well-being to elevated success in a professional context.

Five Categories of Emotional Intelligence (EI/EQ)

Self-awareness is the first step toward introspective self-evaluation. It enables one to identify behavioral and emotional aspects of one's psychological makeup that we can target for change.

Emotional self-awareness is also about recognizing what motivates you and, in turn, what brings you fulfillment.

Self-regulation: the ability to manage one's negative or disruptive emotions and to adapt to changes in circumstance. Those skilled in self-regulation excel in managing conflict, adapt well to change, and are more likely to take responsibility.

Motivation: the ability to self-motivate, focusing on achieving internal or self-gratification instead of external praise or reward. Individuals who can motivate themselves in this way tend to be more committed and goal-focused.

Empathy is recognizing and understanding how others are feeling and considering those feelings before responding to social situations. It also allows an individual to understand the dynamics that influence personal and workplace relationships.

Social skills: the ability to manage the emotions of others through emotional understanding and using this to build rapport and connect with people through skills such as active listening and verbal and nonverbal communication.

Self-awareness is the ability to recognize and understand one's emotions and impact on others.

Emotional intelligence has been shown to play a meaningful role in academic success, mental and physical health, and attainment in professional domains; **Bar-On**'s (1997) findings suggested that *people with higher EI performed better than those with lower EI in life.*

In the modern, agile workplace, employers increasingly

emphasize the importance of EI over academic qualifications. The importance of EI should not go unappreciated; the ability to understand and manage your emotions is the first step in realizing your true potential. How can we achieve meaningful progress if we do not recognize and acknowledge the point from where we are starting? When checking directions on your sat-nav, a destination is useless unless we know the origin.

Emotional intelligence plays a central role in realizing success in both personal and professional life, whether connecting with others and improving interpersonal communication, achieving success in the workplace or social relationships, dealing with stress and improving motivation, or refining decision-making skills.

Self-Management, Self-Regulation, and EQ

While it is commonly accepted that our emotions are driven by impulses over which we have little to no control, we do have the capacity for self-management and self-regulation—the ability to manage—if not control—the resultant emotions and our reactions to them.

Consider the calm and rational pilot despite the aircraft's landing gear being jammed or the surgeon who carries on with their duties despite losing a patient.

This form of self-regulation builds on self-awareness and is an integral part of becoming emotionally intelligent by exercising the capacity to liberate ourselves from impulse-driven reactions (Goleman, 1995).

Self-management builds on this further and allows individuals to use knowledge about their emotions to manage them better, which can help them self-motivate and create positive social interactions.

Leaders with an aptitude for self-regulation are far less likely to be aggressively confrontational and make snap decisions. Self-regulation and self-management do not pertain to the absence of anger; instead, they are about remaining in control of one's emotions and not allowing one's actions to be emotion-driven.

In instances of negative emotions such as anger, EI can help identify what you are feeling and determine the cause through reflection and self-analysis, allowing you to respond rationally. Self-regulation is critical to other facets of EI and can be developed from early childhood, adolescence, and throughout adulthood. Mastering self-management allows us to access the other beneficial aspects of EI, while in the absence of self-regulation, other competencies, such as effective communication and conflict management, are challenging.

The good news is that it is never too late to embark on self-management and regulation training; the potential benefits are numerous and should not be underestimated.

The skills enabled through the development of self-regulation can aid success for (but are not limited to) counselors, psychotherapists, small business owners, managers, and executives.

Those with more vital skills in this area are less likely to become angry or exhibit stress while being more likely to respond calmly to hostile environments, harness personal needs to achieve goals, and remain motivated.

3.3 Emotional Intelligence: The Key to Thriving

"The emotional brain responds to an event more quickly than the thinking brain."
– Daniel Goleman

Value and Benefits of Emotional Intelligence:

The value and benefits of emotional intelligence are vast in terms of personal and professional success. It is a core competency in many vocations, can support advancement towards academic and professional success, improve relationships, and boost communication skills—the list goes on.

Bar-On (1997) suggests that people with higher EI perform better overall than those with lower EI, regardless of IQ. Much discussion has been regarding the benefits of teaching EI in schools, emphasizing that emotionally intelligent children grow up to become emotionally intelligent adults.

Proficiency in EI is becoming a vital prerequisite in prolonged or intense areas of 'emotional work' such as nursing, social work, the service industry, and management roles. High EI improves people's physical and psychological health and encourages academic and business performance (Bar-On & Parker, 2000).

Emotional intelligence is an integral part of forming and developing meaningful human relationships. Schutte et al. (2001) found that, over a series of studies, there were significant links between high EI and more successful interpersonal relations.

Those participants who exhibited higher levels of EI also showed a greater propensity for empathic perspective-taking, cooperation with others, developing affectionate and more satisfying relationships, and greater social skills in general.

So far, we have focused on the social and psychological benefits of EI. It is important to note that self-awareness—the ability to manage emotions and stress—and the ability to solve personal and interpersonal problems are also significantly related to physical health.

Chronic stress and the prolonged adverse effects that accompany it, such as anger, depression, and anxiety, can precipitate the onset and progression of hypertension, heart problems, and diabetes; increase susceptibility to viruses and infections; delay healing of wounds and injuries; and exacerbate conditions such as arthritis and atherosclerosis (Bar-On, 2006; Black & Garbutt, 2002).

The value of EI is immense; developing emotional intelligence encourages many positive traits, from resilience to communication and motivation to stress management, all of which can be seen as conducive to effectively achieving personal, physical, and occupational health and success.

Benefits of Emotional Intelligence:

Undoubtedly, you know how valuable it is to develop your emotional intelligence, but have you ever wondered exactly why?

Research shows many benefits for those with high levels of emotional intelligence, including greater resilience, social skills, and connection.

Resilience and EQ:

Emotional intelligence is undoubtedly a valuable tool for

overcoming adversity; it has the potential to enhance leadership abilities, teamwork effectiveness, and personal resilience.

Focusing on the impact of EI on one's resilience, that is, one's ability to cope with stressful conditions, research suggests that those with higher levels of emotional intelligence are less likely to succumb to the negative impacts of stressors.

In a leadership role, one might expect increased responsibility to coincide with elevated potential stressors, highlighting the importance of strong EI for those in leadership or management positions.

An investigation into the relationship between emotional intelligence and the stress process found that participants who displayed higher levels of EI were less likely to be negatively impacted by the presence of stressors.

In summary, the findings suggested that "EI facets were related to lower threat appraisals, more modest declines in positive affect, less negative affect and challenge physiological responses to stress... This study provides predictive validity that EI facilitates stress resilience" (Schneider et al., 2013, p. 909).

In a nutshell, those with higher levels of emotional intelligence also displayed greater resilience and were less likely to 'burn out' or succumb to depression.

Does Emotional Intelligence Matter More Than IQ?

When psychologists began to discuss intelligence, the focus was on cognitive aspects related to memory and problem-solving.

While there had been references to intelligence as having "non-intellective" as well as "intellective" elements such as affective, personal, and social factors (Wechsler, 1943), historically, the concepts of emotion and intelligence have been regarded as being mutually exclusive. How can one be intelligent about the emotional aspects of life when emotions can hinder individuals from achieving their goals? (Lloyd, 1979).

In reality, high IQ is no guarantee of success. How successful we are in life is determined by both emotional intelligence and IQ, though intellect works best when accompanied by high emotional intelligence.

Goleman (1995, 2011) suggests that IQ versus EI is not simply a case. Instead, both have considerable value. Where IQ tells us the level of cognitive complexity a person can achieve and may, to some degree, predetermine levels of academic achievement, EI tells us which individuals will make the best leaders within top management positions, for example.

IQ has limited connections to work and life success. Snarey and Vaillant (1985) suggested it is less of a predictor of how well we will do in life than our ability to handle frustration, control emotions, and get along with other people—characteristics not only accounted for but also learnable under the current EI theory.

Today, intelligence standards are still commonly applied to cognitive performance. The misconception that IQ alone predicts success is still genuine.

In reality, IQ contributes to around 20% of the factors that determine life success—we all know someone (or perhaps that person) who has a high IQ yet struggles to do 'well.' So, what accounts for the other 80%? Outwitting factors such as social class and plain old luck, Goleman (1995) argued that life success is influenced more by an individual's ability to engage the five aspects of EI detailed above.

While there is much discussion regarding individuals' capability to improve IQ scores, EI can be developed and refined over time if—just like any skill—it is given the necessary focus and effort. Many would argue that the ability to connect with and understand others is a more powerful skill to possess than cognitive intellect alone.

"I've learned that people will forget what you said, what you did, but never how you made them feel."
-Maya Angelou

Is There a Link Between EI and Job Performance?

The increasing awareness of emotional intelligence in management-focused literature and leadership training suggests that the link between emotional intelligence and job performance exists and has value in myriad areas.

The workplace represents a distinct social community, separate from our personal lives. There is a growing appreciation that higher EI allows people to understand themselves better and others, communicate more effectively, and cope with challenging situations.

Utilizing and developing emotional intelligence in the workplace can significantly improve individuals' personal and social capabilities.

EI is about managing emotions to improve job performance

and, in turn, helping people stay calm and think logically to establish good relationships and achieve goals. There is an undeniable relationship between EI and how senior executives manage their employees—managers with higher emotional intelligence have the tools to manage stress and recognize and address it in others.

Emotional intelligence is crucial for managing stress and building relationships. The link between emotional intelligence skills and job performance is clear. Stress management positively impacts job commitment and satisfaction.

It is also important to mention that EI does not only apply at the management level. Likewise, employees lower down the business hierarchy with sophisticated emotional intelligence skills have the desire and ability to establish and maintain high-quality relationships in the workplace (Lopes et al., 2003).

Additionally, individuals with high EI are better equipped to manage conflicts effectively and, in turn, sustain relationships within the workplace than those with low to moderate levels of EI.

Organizations increasingly recognize the value of employees with the skills to cope with change and respond accordingly. EI is an essential factor in job performance on an individual and group level. In fact, as an individual moves up an organizational hierarchy, the positive effect of emotional intelligence on coping with situations and performing tasks effectively increases (Moghadam et al., 2011).

How about Emotional Intelligence and Motivation?

Emotional intelligence matters for motivation, and motivation matters for success. Whether related to work, personal goals, or health, the emotionally intelligent individual understands the deeper meaning of their aspirations and the self-motivation skills required to achieve them.

Goleman (1995) identified four elements of motivation: our drive to improve, our commitment to the goals we set for ourselves, our readiness to act on opportunities that present themselves to us, and our resilience.

Magnano et al. (2016) assert that motivation is the primary psychological process that stimulates us to take action to achieve a desired outcome. Whether picking up the remote to change the TV channel or dedicating hundreds of hours to delivering a project, we would be unable to act without motivation.

Motivation arouses, energizes, directs, and sustains behavior and performance. Intrinsic motivation, which comes from within, pushes us to achieve our full potential. An emotionally intelligent individual possesses the skills for self-motivation and the skills required to motivate others, which is a valuable talent, especially in management positions.

While self-motivation is central to achieving one's goals, emotionally intelligent leaders within a business can also impact employee motivation. The capacity to recognize the emotions and, in turn, the concerns of others is an invaluable skill for realizing the most effective ways to motivate teams and individuals.

A study of senior managers with high EI employed in public sector organizations found that EI augments positive work attitudes, altruistic behavior, and work outcomes. Unsurprisingly, happy employees are motivated employees.

The ability to better cope with stress and anxiety, for example, is also a useful EI tool for motivation—if one can recognize the emotions that may negatively impact motivation, they can be addressed and managed effectively (Carmeli, 2003).

Using Emotional Intelligence to Deal with Stress:

Stress is a common part of our lives, but it's not something we have to let control us. The key is having the right skills, and one of the most powerful tools in this regard is Emotional Intelligence. Those with high Emotional Intelligence are self-aware enough to recognize negative feelings and respond in a way that prevents them from escalating. This is crucial, as uncontrolled and misunderstood emotions can make us more vulnerable to other mental health issues, such as stress, anxiety, and depression.

The skills associated with emotional intelligence can effectively help individuals deal with negative emotional states like stress and promote more positive emotions in their place. Failure to address and manage stress can lead to a further deterioration of one's mental state and, in turn, impact one's physical health.

Research into the social, psychological, and medical components of stress emphasizes the importance of dealing with negative emotions to cope with stress effectively and, in turn, reduce the potential for adverse psychological and physical health outcomes.

Ganster and **Schaubroeck** (1991) consider our working and professional environment as the primary source of stress, suggesting that effectively recognizing and dealing with emotions and emotional information in the workplace is vital in preventing negative stress and coping with occupational

stress.
Emotional intelligence allows us to cope effectively with stress. Furthermore, emotionally intelligent people can initially evaluate situations as less stressful.

Linking EI and Decision-Making:

Emotional Intelligence is closely related to personal and professional development. It impacts more than how we manage our behavior and navigate social complexities; it also affects how we make decisions.

An authentic understanding of our emotions and why we feel them can significantly impact our decision-making abilities. If we cannot look at our emotions objectively, how can we avoid making misguided decisions based on them?

Understanding the causes and consequences of emotions allows individuals to manage their feelings and make objective decisions. Imagine you disagree with your partner and go to work angry and a little stressed out; later that day, you dismiss a proposal from a colleague without really paying attention to what they are suggesting—you are just not in the mood.

This form of emotional interference can be detrimental to the decision-making process. Those with more developed EI can identify and manage this emotional interference and avoid emotionally driven decisions.

Can Emotional Intelligence and Success Be Related?

Much like happiness, ask someone to define success, and you will probably get more than one answer. Does your career make you successful? Your intelligence? How much money do you have? Finding contentment and happiness? Depending on who you ask, it can be anything!

Emotional intelligence can be vital in achieving success, no matter your definition.

As addressed, the most intelligent people do not consistently achieve tremendous success. IQ alone is not enough to excel in life. You can be the most intelligent person in the room, but if you do not have EI, do you have the skills to quiet negative thoughts or the mental fortitude to manage stress? Goleman (1995) described EI as being powerful and, at times, more powerful than IQ in predicting success in life.

Your emotional Intelligence helps you achieve your goals and attain tremendous success. Developing EI can significantly influence our success by increasing morale, motivation, and cooperation (Strickland, 2000).

In the workplace, managers who consistently outperform their peers not only have technical knowledge and experience but, more importantly, utilize the strategies associated with EI to manage conflict, reduce stress, and improve their success.

There is growing evidence that the range of abilities that constitute what is now commonly known as 'emotional intelligence' play a crucial role in determining success—both in one's personal life and the workplace. Real-life applications extend to parenting, relationships, businesses, medical professionals, service workers, etc.

Emotional intelligence enables one to manage emotions in anxiety-provoking situations, such as taking exams at school or university. It is also positively associated with success in personal relationships and social functioning.

Success within social relationships can be achieved by using EI competencies to detect others' emotional states, adopt others' perspectives, enhance communication, and regulate behavior.

Goals and EI:

Let us view goals as personal aspirations. Emotional intelligence skills can be powerful tools for achieving these aspirations when honed. Not only can they help us in our journey, but when leaders and managers apply them effectively, they can also drive significant change and progress in the workplace, benefiting both the individual and the organization.

The facets of emotional intelligence are intricately connected. To reach self-actualization, we must first find motivation. Moreover, to find motivation, we must be content with our actions. Without this contentment, it becomes challenging to muster the motivation needed to achieve our goals. This cycle starts with our emotional well-being and ends with fulfilling our goals. So, how can we expect to achieve our goals without motivation?

A wealth of management literature emphasizes the importance of utilizing EI for success and performance, focusing on how individuals with high EI perform better in all aspects of a management role.

The average level of Emotional Intelligence among team members mirrors the team's process effectiveness and goal focus. In other words, teams with higher EI skills tend to perform at a higher level of goal achievement. This underscores the significant role each individual's emotional intelligence plays in the overall team performance, empowering each team member to contribute to the team's success.

We need positive self-regard, heightened emotional self-awareness, and effective problem-solving and decision-making skills to produce our best and achieve our goals. We must also understand our goals clearly and be motivated to accomplish all we can.

3.4 Building Stronger Connections: Enhancing Social Skills

"The most important single ingredient in the formula of success is knowing how to get along with people."
– Theodore Roosevelt

How does EQ affect communication?

Our ability to be aware of and understand our own emotions can aid our awareness and understanding of the feelings of others.

This sensitivity, or lack thereof, impacts our communication capabilities in both personal and work life.

Let us consider communication in the workplace and, more specifically, conflict resolution. Individuals with higher emotional intelligence are more likely to approach conflict resolution collaboratively, working with others to effectively reach a mutually acceptable outcome.

Relationships in the workplace are affected by how we manage our own emotions and our understanding of the emotions of those around us.

Identifying, managing, and understanding emotions helps us

communicate without confrontation. A person with high EI is better equipped to manage conflict and build meaningful relationships, given their elevated capacity to understand and address the needs of those with whom they engage. (Lopez, 2005).

Emotional intelligence has unquestionably received greater attention in recent years as a driver of effective communication within teams, including the growing area of virtual teams (also known as remote or geographically dispersed teams). Let us examine EQ as a predictor of virtual team success. The results support the idea that not only is EQ a driver of team viability, but it also positively impacts the quality of communication (De Mio, 2002).

Successful communication and, in terms of conflict, successful negotiation are closely linked to high levels of emotional intelligence (EQ). Whereas those with low levels of EQ may react defensively in stressful situations and escalate conflict, individuals with higher emotional intelligence have the skills to communicate effectively without resorting to confrontation or escalating tension.

3.5 The Art of Self-Care: Prioritizing Emotional Well-Being

"While being book-smart might help you pass tests, emotional intelligence prepares you for the real world by being aware of the feelings of others

and your feelings."
— Hannah Owens

Why Emotional Intelligence Matters for Happiness?

Happiness seems like a simple enough concept, but have you ever tried to define it? Try now – what is happiness? It is more complex than it seems because it means something different to us. While it is true that happiness means distinctly different things to different people, it is clear that emotional intelligence matters for happiness, irrespective of your interpretation.

EI facilitators such as happiness contribute to our self-actualization, which contributes to our happiness in a positive feedback loop. According to Wechsler (1943), happiness is the key factor that positively impacts intelligent behavior.

Studies examining the link between EI and a range of interpersonal relations found that participants with higher EQ scores had higher scores for empathic perspective-taking, self-monitoring and social skills, cooperation with partners, relationship satisfaction, and more affectionate relationships. (Schutte, Malouff, Bobik, Coston, Greeson, Jedlicka, Rhodes, & Wendorf, 2001).

By developing the skills for EI, one can reduce stress, which has a positive impact on well-being and happiness. In addition to its motivational value, happiness monitors one's immediate well-being and injects a positive mood into how individuals cope with daily demands, challenges, and pressures.

This positivity encourages the emotional energy required to increase one's motivation to get things done. In short, it helps individuals achieve what they want and tells them how well they are doing (Bar-On, 2001).

Research conducted by Furnham (2003) indicated that a large amount of the variance in happiness and well-being is determined by people's emotion-related self-perceptions and dispositions, such as the ability to regulate emotions, relationship skills, and social competence.

While these EI skills are not the sole contributors to happiness levels, it is essential to recognize their impact. Over 50% of the total variances in happiness are attributed to emotional intelligence competencies.

The emphasis on optimizing happiness has been thoroughly discussed from Aristotle to Freud. To augment happiness, one must often use more sophisticated behavioral patterns, such as self-regulation, to subdue instant pleasure motivations.

Contemporary psychological research continues to recognize the need for this form of optimization. Mischel (1974) explicitly taught children how to delay immediate pleasures for more significant long-term gain. The ability to delay gratification is essential in many aspects of cognitive development, given that the capacity for such delays encourages increased cognitive competence and social maturity.

If we consider happiness and overall life satisfaction, we can agree that developing an aptitude for EI can positively impact well-being and happiness.[31]

3.6 10 Main Takeaways: Self-Compassion:

Cultivating Emotional Intelligence for Success

1. **Emotional Intelligence (EI) Beyond IQ:** Jeffrey Skilling and Kenneth Lay lacked emotional intelligence despite their high IQs, leading to their downfall at Enron. EI involves understanding and managing emotions effectively, which is crucial for making wise decisions and avoiding costly mistakes in personal and professional life.
2. **Components of EI:** EI comprises self-awareness, self-regulation, motivation, empathy, and social skills. These components empower individuals to navigate challenges, manage stress, build relationships, and focus on long-term goals rather than short-term gains.
3. **Self-Regulation**: Mastering self-regulation allows individuals to control impulses, manage negative emotions like anger, and respond thoughtfully rather than impulsively. This skill is essential for effective leadership and personal grow.
4. **Practical Strategies**: Techniques like mindfulness, self-reflection, and recognizing physiological cues can help enhance self-awareness and self-regulation, contributing to overall emotional intelligence.
5. **Benefits of EI**: Research indicates that EI is more predictive of success than IQ in various life domains, including academic achievement, career advancement, and personal relationships. Investing in EI development can improve decision-making, interpersonal skills, and overall well-being.

6. **Professional and Personal Success**: EI is a critical skill for success across various fields, enhancing resilience, social skills, and leadership effectiveness. Research underscores its role in better job performance, stress management, and fostering positive workplace relationships.
7. **Relationships and Communication**: High EI fosters better interpersonal relations by improving empathy, conflict resolution, and communication. Individuals with higher EI are adept at managing emotions, which enhances their ability to connect meaningfully with others.
8. **Stress Management**: EI equips individuals with tools to recognize and manage stress effectively, improving mental and physical well-being. This skill is crucial in high-pressure environments like workplaces.
9. **Decision-Making and Motivation**: EI enhances decision-making by helping individuals manage emotional interference. It also boosts intrinsic motivation, which is vital for achieving personal and professional goals.
10. **Happiness and Well-Being**: Emotional intelligence significantly improves self-awareness, relationship satisfaction, and stress reduction, enhancing life satisfaction and well-being.

Chapter 4: Rewiring Your Brain: Unraveling the Neuroscience of Change

4.1 Your Brain on Change: The Neuroscience of Transformation

"The brain is wider than the sky."
– Emily Dickinson

The human brain is often considered the most complex object in the known universe. It has around 100 billion neurons, roughly the same number of stars in the Milky Way, and ten quadrillion connections (the number ten followed by fifteen zeros). If we used our best brain-imaging technology, it would take dozens of our most advanced microscopes, working around the clock, thousands of years to collect the data required to map out the wiring of the nervous system with synapse-level detail [3]. Any new insights into the actual workings of this complex apparatus are bound to offer breakthroughs for humanity. [32]

The mysteries of the mind are many and complex, but neuroscience is beginning to unravel some of them. Neuroplasticity, or the ability to rewire your brain, is one that I am particularly interested in. Extensive studies by neuroscientists confirm that mental processes can alter brain matter's physical structure – neural networks in particular. This is excellent news for those of us who struggle to make good habits stick, regardless of how badly we want to make positive choices.[33]

According to the esteemed **Dr. Jeffrey Schwartz, a research psychiatrist and one of the world's leading experts in neuroplasticity**, author of the book ***Brain Lock***, here is a look at his method, which he has confirmed can be used to positively create change in any area of our personal or professional lives.

1. Relabel Thoughts as Deceptive Brain Experiences:

According to **Schwartz**, the first step to rewiring your brain is to label a ***thought***, ***feeling***, or ***behavior*** to help you recognize it for what it is.

For example, if an unwanted thought creeps in, you might relabel it as a ***"false message"*** or ***"brain glitch."*** This process helps you train yourself to avoid being tricked by automatic thought patterns, feelings, and behaviors. You can step back and say, "This is just my brain sending me a false message." (Someone with OCD, obsessive-compulsive disorder, might say, "I have a compulsive urge to check the stove" instead of "I have to check the stove.")

This process can be more complicated than it seems. The point is to mindfully understand superficial, involuntary brain habits at a deep, neurological level.

Next time you are struggling to come up with a new idea and impulsively assume, *"I am not creative enough to solve this problem," consider labeling that unhelpful thought for what it is: an uncomfortable sensation that makes you feel like you are not capable, even if you are.*

2. Reattribute the Thought to Its Real Source:

The second step to help successfully rewire your brain focuses on answering the question, *"Why do these thoughts and tendencies keep coming back?" The true answer is almost always, "It is not me; it is my brain!" The brain can misfire, get stuck in gear, create mental noise, and send false messages – all out of years of engrained habit or even clinically dysfunctional neural networks (as in the case of OCD).* If you understand why unhelpful thought patterns or habits are constantly popping up, you may eventually be able to recognize that they are ***"brain glitches"*** that you can manually override.

Say a lifelong procrastinator keeps postponing a critical project. This is an excellent opportunity to assess why they tend to put it off rather than get it done. Maybe they think they are bored, but it is just an excuse to avoid getting started. Alternatively, maybe they have perfectionist tendencies and are afraid of failure. Regardless of the rationale, they can start to rewire the brain by reattributing the setback to its actual source: *Procrastination often results from a battle between the prefrontal cortex (the part of the brain responsible for complex planning and decision-making) and the limbic system (the part of the brain that says do what feels good, now). Generally, the prefrontal cortex is less developed than the limbic system, so the "feel good" part of the brain often wins, perpetuating the cycle of procrastination. In other words, it is your brain, not you.*

That raises the natural next question: What can you do about it?

3. Refocus Your Mind by Shifting to a Positive Activity:

The third step to rewiring your brain is usually the toughest, requiring changing your behavior. According to **Schwartz**'s method, *this involves directing your attention toward a productive or wholesome activity despite false or deceptive thoughts. For example, refuse to be misled by unhelpful messages – "I am not creative enough to solve this problem" – and instead go for a brief walk or refocus on a hobby you enjoy. This can give you the time and space to help you recognize that automatic thought patterns can be invalid. When you refocus, your mind can take charge of your brain, allowing you to begin changing your mindset at a neurochemical level.*

It is like manually shifting the gears of a car. "The automatic transmission is not working, so you manually override it," says Schwartz. "With positive, desirable alternatives – they can be anything you enjoy and can do consistently every time – you are repairing the gearbox. The more you do it, the smoother the shifting becomes. Like most other things, the more you practice, the easier and more natural it becomes because your brain is beginning to function more efficiently, calling up the new pattern without thinking about it."

4. Revalue Your Thoughts for What They Objectively Are:

The rewiring process all comes together in the fourth step, which is the combined effect of the first three steps. When you ***relabel***, ***reattribute***, and ***refocus***, your brain creates a ***new connection***. Repeating these actions can reinforce the connection. As a result, you can begin to ***"revalue"*** old patterns as distractions or habits engrained within the brain. You can assess how accurate or valid those thoughts are, what would happen if you gave in to them, and what you want to achieve instead of falling back on the habits you want to break. In turn, patterns that once held you back become deceptive brain messages with little value. As you work on rewiring your brain over time, the old tendencies can begin to fade in intensity altogether.

Then, ***"two very positive things happen,"*** Schwartz says. *"The first is that you are happier because you have control over your behavioral response to your thoughts and feelings. The second thing is that you change the faulty brain chemistry by doing that."*

The Bottom Line:

Schwartz confirmed that although he is focused on treating OCD, his methods could be used to rewire the brain to create change in any area of business, work, or life. *"Since it has been scientifically demonstrated that the brain has been altered through the behavior change, it is safe to say that you could do the same thing by altering responses to any other behaviors." This means we can improve our ability to defeat the mental traps we fall into, especially when facing a challenge*. [34]

This repetitive process changes the structures of our brain, which are measurable.

This process can be facilitated by mindfulness and meditation. The ***amygdala***, an almond-shaped structure necessary for emotional processing, can change. Being mindful can reduce its size because it buffers stress seen in the amygdala. *When* *you experience increased stress, the level of cortisol increases and remains high. It can become toxic for your brain. Stress can directly inhibit neuroplasticity.*

The other physical change is to the ***cingulate cortex***, part of the limbic system involved in our behavioral and emotional responses. It is also essential for the default mode network (DMN). A region that becomes active when the mind wanders and contemplates.[35]

4.2 Rewiring Your Brain: Strategies for Neural Plasticity

"Neurons that fire together wire together."
-Donald Hebb

By the time you finish this sub-chapter, your brain will be different.

This cerebral shift is neuroplasticity—the brain's ability to change and restructure. Every time the brain processes new information, neurons fire, new pathways form, and the malleable brain alters its shape and structure.

In recent years, several researchers have posited that it is possible to consciously direct neuroplasticity to optimize brain function, improve work performance, and influence team performance.

Once you understand how neuroplasticity works, you will discover that the concept is much more straightforward than it sounds.

What is neuroplasticity?

In a nutshell, neuroplasticity is the brain's ability to learn and adapt. Until recently, experts believed that our brains were fixed by the end of adolescence and that, in terms of neurons, it was all downhill from there. *However, the latest research has proved that our brains can grow and change throughout adulthood. That is, if we treat our neural pathways correctly. "The main point of neuroplasticity is that you can form and reorganize connections in your brain,"* says **Dr. Marsha Chinichian**, a ***Los Angeles-based clinical psychotherapist*** and the brains behind the acclaimed mental fitness app ***Mindshine***. [36]

"For a long time, we thought that humans were born with many neurons, synapses, and connections, and as we age, they simply die off. However, we have learned that this is not true. We can make changes to develop our brains further. We have learned we can rewire our brains."

Dr. Chinichian's enthusiasm is echoed by leading cognitive experts worldwide, including **Natalia Ramsden**, a business psychologist and founder of ***SOFOS Associates*** in London, the UK's first and only brain optimization clinic.

"There is something hugely empowering about the idea that we, as individuals, can change the structure of our brains for the better," says Ramsden. "There is so much we can do to develop their function, which in turn can dramatically increase our productivity in the workplace."

Make better decisions and prevent cognitive fatigue—that is the concept of neuroplasticity.

However, how do we implement it in our daily working lives?

Imagine your brain as a colossal power grid. Billions of pathways light up whenever you think, feel, or do something. Putting neuroplasticity into action means carving new pathways while strengthening the best of the existing ones – and not reinforcing the pathways you would rather avoid. This is captured in an aphorism: ***"Neurons that fire together, wire together; neurons that fire out of synch fail to link."***

Neuroscientist **Dr. Tara Swart**, a senior lecturer at MIT and author of the bestselling brain bible ***The Source***, recently compared this process to road building.

"Think of it as going from a dirt road to a motorway," Dr. Swart told European CEO [37]

. *"I could say, 'I am going to work on that pathway, which is currently a dirt road. The more I use it, and the more I repeat activities, I can build it up to a motorway.'"*

That newly built motorway will help you process information faster and better equip you to relieve mental fatigue. That means less stress and fewer mistakes.

"It can help to think of your brain in terms of a muscle," says **Dr. Lynda Shaw**, a ***chartered psychologist and cognitive neuroscientist*** who is a ***Fellow of The Royal Society of Medicine and an Associate Fellow of the British Psychological Society. "If you do enough bicep curls, you will increase the size of your biceps. It is the same process with your brain. If you exercise your brain correctly and often, neuroplasticity means it will become more powerful."***

From a remote working perspective, experts say that neuroplasticity is an even more valuable tool as daily office stimuli dramatically decrease and new routines and rituals emerge.

"We need, as bosses, to encourage our people to embrace change and adapt by being innovative and creative," says **Dr. Shaw**. ***"Neuroplasticity is a great way of doing that and of teams staying ahead of that curve."***

Below are some tips by experts for harnessing the power of neuroplasticity for yourself.

Nine techniques to "rewire" your cognitive pathways:

1. Feed your brain

Your brain makes up only a tiny proportion of your body weight but uses up a quarter of everything you eat. If you want enhanced neural pathways, you will need an enhanced diet. According to Ramsden, that means grabbing snacks like walnuts, blueberries, and avocado during the day. *Vitamin D and magnesium are top priorities if you want to promote neuroplasticity.*

2. Take naps

A good night's sleep between seven and nine hours will always prepare you for a better brain day. *However, a short afternoon nap of around 20 minutes will elevate your neuroplasticity potential even further. A short nap encourages the growth of dendritic spines, which act as crucial connectors between the neurons in your brain.*

3. Do not let the work day linger

Like muscle-building, neuroplasticity needs downtime to do its work correctly. According to **Dr. Chinichian**, managers should embed and enforce a ***"close the day"*** ritual that prioritizes reflection and gratitude for small wins. An end-of-day Slack message saying, *"Thanks for the great ideas in the brainstorming session today, everyone. See you tomorrow"* can help the team feel valued. Putting a hard stop to the day's stresses in a way that also boosts endorphins creates perfect conditions for neuroplasticity. Bonus: It also signals that it is OK to ***"leave"*** work and unplug for the evening.

4. Expand your vocabulary

Try to learn one new word every day. According to experts, this simple act will spark many new neural pathways, both visual and auditory. (*Give it a few months, and it will make you unstoppable at Scrabble, too).*

5. Use the "wrong" hand

Non-dominant hand exercises are excellent for forming new neural pathways and strengthening the connectivity between existing neurons. *For instance, if you are right-handed, try brushing your teeth with your left hand – and then try it while balancing on one leg for a double neuroplasticity bonus.*

6. Learn to juggle

Juggling is frequently cited as an excellent means for improving neuroplasticity. *Keep a small set of balls in your work drawer for a brain boost whenever you have a few spare seconds between tasks.* The better you get, the bigger the benefits.

7. Play chess

Indulge your inner Beth Harmon by embracing chess – a game that has endless potential for neuroplasticity. *Chess players have significantly more grey matter in their anterior cingulate cortex than those unfamiliar with en passant and castling. Moreover, you do not even need another player or a board to reap the mental benefits.* Log onto **chess.com** for a quick blast whenever you have a few minutes. (*You do not need to finish a game to get the neurological boost.)*

8. *Do mnemonic drills*

Teaching yourself mnemonic devices, like formulas or rhymes, can enhance connectivity in your prefrontal parietal network, paving the way to new, positive pathways in your brain. Get started here.[38]

9. *Be mindful, as a team*

The clinician says that one of the best things you can do to promote neuroplasticity in a workforce is to incorporate regular group meditation. There are multiple online options available to get you started, like this [39]

and this. Not only does it help with the positive brain rewiring process (while expanding several valuable parts of the brain), but it results in team members reacting to problems with an increased sense of calm, passion, and awareness. Neuroplasticity at its finest.[40]

4.3 The Role of Dopamine and Serotonin in Motivation and Happiness

"Dopamine is the brain's reward and pleasure chemical." – Anonymous

During my M. Tech days at IIT(ISM), Dhanbad, India, there used to be a tea stall called Ramadhani on campus. It is still there and can be found on Google Maps. It was under a big banyan tree whose shadow covered the stall, keeping its surroundings cool. It remains open 24x7. Students can be found taking tea and snacks there around the clock.

We two friends were having tea during the break after the second-semester results were declared, and we both were very comfortable maintaining our grades. After all, we had worked hard, especially in the month preceding the semester exam. We were planning a short break. We planned to visit our native villages. We recalled our childhood and all those stupid things we might have done then and laughed continuously. It was in my mind that I would show my three-year-old son my primary school in my village.

Suddenly, some unknown person came to us and directly told my friend that his father had had a severe road accident and was struggling for his life in the hospital. He, being the only son, burst into tears. It was tough for me and that man to control him. The man belonged to his village.

It is an experience that most people come across as being entirely unprepared to handle in life – from well-deserved happiness to sad moments in a fraction of a second.

Is it not?

You are stuck.

You do not understand what makes what and why.

You instantaneously attribute such things as a curse or something for which only you are to blame.

It may be nothing of that shot.

Let us delve deep into ***happiness*** and ***motivation***.

Signs of Happiness

While people's perceptions of happiness may differ, psychologists look for critical signs when measuring and assessing happiness.

Some key signs of happiness include:

- Feeling like you are living the life you wanted
- Going with the flow and a willingness to take life as it comes
- Feeling that the conditions of your life are good
- Enjoying positive, healthy relationships with other people
- Feeling that you have accomplished (or will accomplish) what you want in life
- Feeling satisfied with your life
- Feeling positive more than negative
- Being open to new ideas and experiences
- Practicing self-care and treating yourself with kindness and compassion
- Experiencing gratitude
- Feeling that you are living life with a sense of meaning and purpose
- Wanting to share your happiness and joy with others

One important thing to remember is that happiness is not a state of constant euphoria. Instead, happiness is an overall sense of experiencing more positive emotions than negative ones.

Happy people still feel the whole range of human emotions—anger, frustration, boredom, loneliness, and even sadness—from time to time. However, even when faced with discomfort, they have an underlying sense of optimism that things will get better, that they can deal with what is happening, and that they can feel happy again.

"Even people who have experienced terrible trauma can still also experience happiness," says **Hannah Owens**, **LMSW**, *"though it is important to recognize that it might be more difficult for them to obtain the balance generally associated with overall happiness and that their happiness might look very different from others' who have not had to deal with such challenges."* [41]

Happiness's underlying factors are important from two dimensions:

Endogenic factors (biological, cognitive, personality, and ethical sub-factors) and

Exogenic factors (behavioral, sociocultural, economic, geographical, life events, and aesthetics sub-factors).

Among all endogenic factors, biological sub-factors are significant predictors of happiness. The existence of significant differences in temperament and happiness of infants is an indicator of biological influences.

Studies on genetic factors have indicated that genetics is practical, on average, in improving happiness by about 35 - 50 percent. Despite difficulties finding particular genes, several genes are distributed in emotion and mood.

Neuroscience studies showed that some parts of the brain (e.g., **amygdala**, **hippocampus**, and **limbic system**) and neurotransmitters (e.g., **dopamine**, **serotonin**, **norepinephrine**, and **endorphin**) play a role in controlling happiness. A few studies pointed to the role of **cortisol**, **adrenaline (adrenal gland**), and **oxytocin (pituitary**

gland) in controlling happiness. Physical health and typology also concluded in most related studies to have a significant role in happiness. Therefore, according to previous research, it can be said that biological and health factors are critical in underlying happiness, and their role in happiness is undeniable.

Some researchers believe that happiness is due to genetic and inherited factors, and others believe that happiness is caused by environmental factors like high income, education, and being active during life. Results of previous studies suggest that just one or two factors do not cause happiness but result from integrating several factors. As a whole, two general factors influence emotions in individuals. Happiness is an emotion formed as a general interaction between internal (endogenic) and external (exogenic) factors.

Brain and Neurotransmitters

The brain manages all the activities: thoughts, feelings, activities, learning, and love. Mood and emotions are not acceptable for this role.

"The brain's emotion circuitry is complex, primarily involving structures in the prefrontal cortex, amygdala, hippocampus, anterior cingulated cortex, and insular cortex. These structures normally work together to process and generate emotional information and behavior. Research has particularly focused on the prefrontal cortex, which, unlike most other brain regions involved in emotion processing, shows asymmetric activation about positive and negative emotions" [42]

On the other hand, studies have shown that positive and negative moods are affected by brain chemicals in several ways. Two of the most important neurotransmitters involved in mood are **dopamine** and **serotonin**. Positive mood and negative mood are mediated by dopamine and serotonin levels.[43]

Dopamine and serotonin are chemical messengers, or neurotransmitters, that help regulate many bodily functions.

People sometimes refer to dopamine and serotonin as the "happy hormones" because they regulate mood and emotion.

They are also involved in several mental health conditions, including low mood and depression.

Dopamine and serotonin are involved in similar bodily processes but operate differently. Imbalances of these chemicals can cause different medical conditions that require different treatments.

What is dopamine?

Neurons in the brain release dopamine, which carries signals between neurons.

The body uses dopamine to create chemicals called norepinephrine and epinephrine.

Dopamine is integral to the reward system, a group of brain processes that control motivation, desire, and cravings.

Dopamine levels also influence the following bodily functions:

- ***Mood***
- ***Sleep***
- ***Learning***
- ***Movement***
- ***Alertness***
- ***blood flow***

- ***urine output***

What is serotonin?

Serotonin is another neurotransmitter present in the brain.

However, roughly 95%Trusted Source of the body's total serotonin resides in the enterochromaffin cells in the gut, where it helps regulate the movement of the digestive system.

In addition to aiding digestion, serotonin is involved in regulating:

- ***the sleep-wake cycle***
- ***mood and emotions***
- ***metabolism and appetite***
- ***cognition and concentration***
- ***hormonal activity***
- ***body temperature***
- ***blood clotting***

Differences between dopamine and serotonin

Although dopamine and serotonin relay messages between neurons and affect mood and concentration, they have other distinct functions.

Dopamine, for example, relays signals between neurons that control body movements and coordination.

This neurotransmitter is a trusted source in the brain's pleasure and reward center and drives many behaviors. Eating certain foods, taking illegal drugs, and engaging in behaviors such as gambling can all cause dopamine levels in the brain to spike.

Higher dopamine levels can lead to euphoria, bliss, and

enhanced motivation and concentration. Therefore, exposure to substances and activities that increase dopamine can become addictive to some individuals.

Like dopamine, serotonin can influence people's moods and emotions, but it also helps regulate Trusted Source digestive functions, such as appetite, metabolism, and gut motility.

Similarities between dopamine and serotonin

Both dopamine and serotonin are neurotransmitters with positive associations.

They are also neuromodulators, meaning that, unlike other neurotransmitters, they can communicate with many neurons near and far from the dopamine or serotonin release site.

As neuromodulators, dopamine, and serotonin also send signals that last longer than the signals of other neurotransmitters.

The relationship between dopamine and serotonin

Neurotransmitters do not act independently. They interact with and affect each other to maintain a careful chemical balance within the body. There are strong structural and functional links between the serotonin and dopamine systems.

Which conditions have links to dopamine and serotonin?

Having abnormal levels of either dopamine or serotonin can lead to several different medical conditions.

Both neurotransmitters can affect mood disorders, such as depression. Imbalances can also result in distinct conditions that affect different bodily functions.

The following sections cover these conditions in more detail.

Dopamine

Dopamine deficiency may play a significant role in the following conditions and symptoms:

- ***Parkinson's disease***
- ***Depression***
- ***Schizophrenia***
- ***Hallucinations***
- ***Dopamine also plays a role in motivation and reward-driven behaviors.***

The SLC6A3 ***gene-trusted*** Source provides instructions for creating the dopamine transporter protein. This protein transports dopamine molecules across neuron membranes.

A medical condition that health experts call dopamine transporter deficiency syndrome or infantile parkinsonism-dystonia occurs when mutations in the SLC6A3 gene affect how the dopamine transporter protein functions.

Dopamine transporter deficiency syndrome disrupts dopamine signaling, which impacts the body's ability to regulate movement.

For this reason, dopamine transporter deficiency syndrome produces symptoms similar to those of Parkinson's disease, ***including-Trusted*** Sources:

- ***tremors, spasms, and cramps in the muscles***

- ***difficulty eating, swallowing, speaking, and moving***
- ***impaired coordination and dexterity***
- ***involuntary or unusual eye movements***
- ***decreased facial expression, or hypomimia***
- ***difficulty sleeping***
- ***frequent pneumonia infections***
- ***digestive issues, such as acid reflux and constipation***

Read on to learn more about dopamine and Parkinson's disease.

Serotonin

Having too much serotonin can lead to a potentially life-threatening medical condition called serotonin syndrome or serotonin toxicity.

This condition can occur after taking too much of a serotonergic medication or taking multiple serotonergic medications at the same time.

Aside from selective serotonin reuptake inhibitors (SSRIs), other serotonergic medications can include-Trusted Source:

- ***serotonin and norepinephrine reuptake inhibitors, such as venlafaxine***
- ***tricyclic antidepressants, such as desipramine and imipramine***
- ***certain migraine medications, including almotriptan and rizatriptan***

Do dopamine and serotonin make a person happy?

Dopamine and serotonin are also called the “happy hormones” because they promote mental well-being.

Dopamine, the “feel-good” hormone, is associated with the brain’s reward system and produces pleasant sensations.

Serotonin can help increase happiness by alleviating depression and anxiety.[44]

History of Happiness

Happiness has long been recognized as a critical part of health and well-being. The "pursuit of happiness" is even given as an inalienable right in the U.S. Declaration of Independence. However, our understanding of what will bring happiness has shifted over time.

Psychologists have also proposed several theories to explain how people experience and pursue happiness. These theories include:

Maslow's Hierarchy of Needs [45]

The hierarchy of needs suggests that people are motivated to pursue increasingly complex needs. Once more basic needs are fulfilled, people are motivated by more psychological and emotional needs.

At the peak of the hierarchy is the need for self-actualization, or the need to achieve one's full potential. The theory also stresses the importance of peak experiences or transcendent moments in which a person feels deep understanding, happiness, and joy.

Positive Psychology

The pursuit of happiness is central to the field of positive psychology. Psychologists who study positive psychology are interested in learning ways to increase positivity and help people live happier, more satisfying lives. [46]

4.4The Science of Habit Formation: Breaking Bad Habits

"We are what we repeatedly do. Excellence, then, is not an act but a habit."
– Aristotle

Imagine someone who has a ***"bad"*** habit of smoking, and that person wants to develop a ***"good"*** habit of working out. What would reasonably be the easiest thing to do: changing clothes, preparing a bag, driving 10 minutes to the gym, and getting a workout of over an hour doing, or smoking a cigarette when it is right there on the table after the boss yelled at him?

What do you think is more rewarding? To work out a few days a week without seeing results or to smoke a cigarette and immediately calm down for a few minutes after a stressful day?

Do you see what I am talking about?

<u>*Getting out of our comfort zone and breaking bad habits is always more challenging because our bad habits are more comfortable than the good ones that improve our lives. Therefore, if we reverse the situation, we can*</u>

quickly form better habits and eliminate bad ones.
The simple answer to this ***"complex problem"*** is that we need to simplify the good habits that we would like to build so that they are more straightforward for our brain to identify as something it would like to repeat.

Want to work out more?

Please find a way to make it more fun, like doing it with a friend or listening to your favorite playlist.

Want to stop playing on the PlayStation so much?

Please find a way to make it hard to access it in the first place, like plugging it out after each use so that you will have to plug all the cables back in the next time you want to play.

Be creative. After some time, the habit of making and breaking habits will be inherent in you.

Why is it so hard to develop and maintain good habits?

Because your brain will resist the change.

Your brain, indeed, loves habits.

Why?

Because they repeat certain behaviors over time, the more you repeat them, the more your brain uses them. Chances are that you are already practicing many daily habits, even if you are unaware of them.

Scroll through TikTok videos on your phone as soon as you wake up.

Brushing your teeth from top to bottom or left to right.

We are preparing the same type of breakfast each morning.

You are choosing your favorite spices to add to a meal.

Also, bad habits when stressed are biting your nails,

lighting a cigarette, taking a second beer out of the fridge, helping yourself to more potato chips, and staying up half the night watching TV.

All of those behaviors — whether you think they are good or bad — are habits.

When you start practicing a new habit you believe to be good for you, your brain resists. It is as if it is telling you: Why are you getting up so early? We like it here in this warm bed! Why don't you have another piece of cake? It tastes so good, and you deserve it after working so hard this week. Why go to bed now? The couch feels comfortable, and this show is entertaining to watch!

To overcompensate for this brain resistance, you devise different ways to make your habit stick. You start to be extra hard on yourself by setting goals that are too unrealistic, too much, too soon. I have to lose 10 pounds in one month. I want to read one book a day for the rest of the year. I have to quit smoking right now. I have to start getting up at 5 a.m.

Moreover, what happens next?

You start the new habit and feel good about it for a while because the motivation kicks in. However, your brain is still stuck in its ways, so you feel discomfort as you repeat the new behavior. Sooner or later, your brain signals — we have had enough! One morning, you are not motivated to get up early and go for that run. You start berating yourself first, then return to your usual, comfortable sleeping routine. Moreover, the new habit disappears.

If you want to get your brain on board with practicing a new good habit, I suggest the following:

Do not make the change too obvious. Do not be too demanding, too ambitious, or too unrealistic initially.

Instead

1. ***Keep it simple.***

It is so simple that all you should do is start with tiny steps. Do a mini-workout at home for 10 minutes this month. Find a healthy and simple breakfast idea you can execute in 5 minutes or less. Go to bed 15 minutes earlier than usual to give yourself time to de-stress and relax with a good book, even if that means reading ten pages.

2. ***Practice early in the day.***

We all have a finite amount of willpower that takes us through the day, so if you want to focus on your top priority—your new habit—work on it early. Practice a new skill before lunchtime while you are still energized and focused. If you are focused on creativity, practice sketching, painting, or writing for one hour. Do not leave these activities for late at night when you might feel exhausted from the day.

3. ***Repeat.***

Why? If you practice it once or twice a week, it is less likely you will make any habit stick. Your brain will start thinking this is an optional activity, not a necessary one. You will get better results if you start doing it more frequently, so your brain gets accustomed to it and eventually adopts the new behavior as a regular part of the day. How can you do this? Schedule it in a daily planner or add it to your mobile phone monthly calendar, then set a notification to remind you an hour or two ahead of time when to start.

4. ***Think of your new habit as a choice, not a***

chore.

When you start doing something different, ask yourself, why am I doing this? What will this new behavior afford me? Staying connected to the initial reason for picking the new habit is essential. Maybe you want to work out to improve your health and lose weight. Alternatively, maybe you want to work on creative skills like bread-making or playing guitar. Think about how you will feel after you have succeeded in making this habit a part of your everyday life. Choosing a positive behavior will make you feel more robust, powerful, and proactive.

5. ***The urge to quit*.**

The writer **Seth Godin** said, never quit something with great long-term potential just because you cannot deal with the stress of the moment. It is essential to stop for a minute and be aware of your stress and where it is coming from. If keeping a new habit is stressing you out, figure out why. Eating healthy meals is difficult if your housemates binge on pizza every night. Alternatively, accepting that you are not the fittest, most productive, or well-read person in your circle of friends is tough. That is OK. Fight the urge to give up when things get tough. Know what feels hard right now and what is good for you in the long run. Moreover, if you have a bad day, be patient with yourself. Tomorrow, get after it again and keep moving forward. Day after day.[47]

Developing and maintaining good habits can be challenging for several reasons:

1. ***Initial Effort***: Establishing a new habit requires significant effort and discipline. Breaking out of old routines and pushing yourself to adopt new behaviors can be challenging.

2. ***Consistency***: Habits require consistency to stick. Maintaining a new habit daily can be difficult, especially when faced with distractions, stress, or competing priorities.

3. ***Instant Gratification vs. Long-Term Benefits***: Good habits often provide long-term benefits but may not offer immediate rewards. It can be hard to stay motivated when the results of your efforts are not immediately apparent.

4. ***Lack of Accountability:*** Without external accountability or support, giving up on a habit can be easy when faced with obstacles or setbacks.

5. ***Environmental Factors:*** Your environment can play a significant role in shaping your habits. If your surroundings do not support the behavior you are trying to adopt, it can be challenging to maintain the habit.

6. ***Lack of Planning***: Failing to plan for obstacles or setbacks can make it harder to stick to a new habit. It is easy to fall back into old patterns without a clear strategy.

7. ***Self-Doubt and Negative Self-Talk***: Negative self-talk or self-doubt can undermine your efforts to develop good habits. Cultivating a positive mindset and believing in your ability to change is essential.

8. ***Overambitious Goals***: Setting unrealistic or overly ambitious goals can set you up for failure. It is essential to start small and gradually build on your successes to create

lasting habits.

9. Lack of Motivation: Without a strong reason or motivation for adopting a new habit, it can be challenging to stay committed when faced with obstacles or temptations.

10. Lack of Patience: Developing good habits takes time and patience. It is essential to recognize that change does not happen overnight and to forgive yourself when you slip up.

By understanding these challenges and taking proactive steps to address them, such as setting specific goals, creating a supportive environment, and building accountability, you can increase your chances of successfully developing and maintaining good habits. [48]

Habit creation is an integral part of living a better life. It comes about through instrumental learning, which will be repeated if one's response is rewarded. Habits are learned behaviors that become automatic responses when they have been consistently carried out in the same context over time. It can take some effort to form new healthy patterns, but once achieved, this pays off immensely as these behaviors often continue without conscious thought or control.

The Habit Loop (Fig.1)

The habit formation process is often called the 'habit loop.' It involves three main steps: an initial cue that triggers a behavior and a ***sequence of activities*** that culminates in receiving some ***reward***. This cyclical mechanism plays a vital role in forming habits because they become more embedded if done consistently and frequently with sufficient self-control.

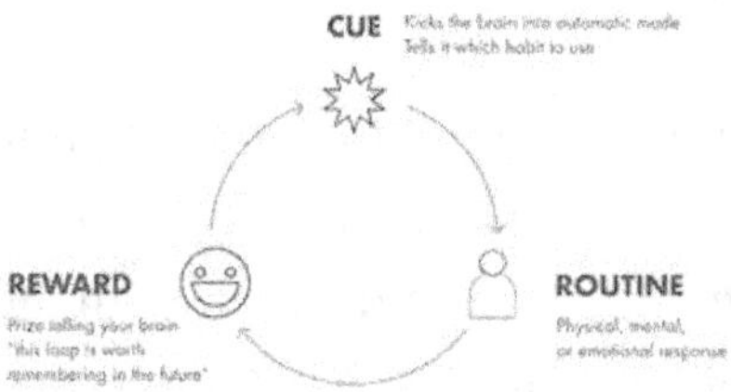

Fig.1

This dynamic can also lead people into action without consciously reflecting on their decisions, resulting in habitual responses that are part of our daily routine. Understanding how these processes work can help us recognize cues, routines, and rewards associated with bad habits and replace them with healthier alternatives over time.

Factors Influencing Bad Habits

Bad habits develop through the habit formation process, in which behaviors become automatic over time. This can be exacerbated by stress and lead to drug addiction due to goal-directed choices being replaced with chronic ones. Habit slips happen when a person engages unintentionally in an established behavior based on their environment or action cues. To make change possible, it is beneficial to identify factors that influence bad habits while also making healthy alternatives visible and accessible for people working towards replacing harmful practices with positive ones within the context of the so-called habit loop.'

Strategies for Breaking Bad Habits

We must determine the prompts that cause bad habits and replace our old behaviors with new ones to combat them. Investigating potential environmental cues can give us insight into these triggers. Concentrating on one habit at a time is usually adequate for replacing undesired routines. This may be an encouraging way of staying motivated as you strive to improve and break your negative patterns. Setting objectives and tracking progress will also help inspire you while working towards eliminating those detrimental practices over time.

Identifying Triggers

The first step in attempting to break a bad habit is recognizing what triggers it. Both internal and external factors may be at play in promoting this behavior. Internal stimuli, such as emotions or the time of day, come from within us. In contrast, environmental cues can automatically cause specific actions, like reaching for an unhealthy snack while shopping.

Tracking your activities in a journal or using apps that track habits makes patterns more accessible to notice and use. With a proper understanding of the related triggers behind them, new routines can replace old ones more easily.

Replacing Bad Habits

One way to overcome unwanted habits is to swap them for more beneficial ones. This strategy involves shifting the routine associated with a habit without altering its cue and reward elements. For instance, if feeling pressured contributes to poor snacking choices, replacing snacks with activities such as walking or practicing relaxation techniques could be an option.

Habitual behaviors can also cease during significant changes like switching jobs or relocating; these scenarios cause less contact with cues that fuel old habits, allowing us to break habit loops and substitute bad practices for superior alternatives.

Maintaining Progress

To stay motivated and see progress in breaking bad habits, you must track your behavior and any situations or activities that lead up to the habit. Keeping a journal of what occurs can help pinpoint potential triggers and patterns in how you behave. It is also essential to set realistic goals for yourself once achieved. Instead of relying on alcohol consumption, they are rewarded with something like an activity they enjoy; such rewards will aid in staying dedicated to combatting problematic behaviors and retaining positive ones.

Developing Good Habits

Forming good habits starts with understanding the habit-formation process and mastering self-control. It is vital to create a supportive environment for success. In this section, we will advise how to distinguish between helpful and unhelpful habits, strengthen willpower, and build an encouraging social circle around oneself.

Recognizing which activities are advantageous is often tricky but very important to developing effective behaviors that will last over time. Establishing desirable routines requires firm resolve since it facilitates one's ability to resist undesirable behavior patterns or impulses.

Habit Formation Process:

Developing a habit has three distinct phases: ***initiation, learning****, and* ***stability****. Repetition plays a vital role in reinforcing the new behavior; research demonstrated that it can take up to 254 days of regular practice to transform something into a daily ritual without any additional effort or thought involved.*

Forming habits is not overly complex. All you need is dedication and consistency when carrying out specific activities within particular contexts, for they eventually become autonomous actions through automaticity development during the learning period, leading to eventual stabilization where one will no longer have difficulty maintaining their newly instilled behaviors with ease.

Building Self-Control:

One way to develop self-control is by having objectives, practicing mindfulness, and establishing a solid support network. One should create strategies to avert temptations while concentrating on defined aims and the effects of their actions. Physical exercise combined with eating healthy meals and getting adequate sleep helps increase focus and overall health, enabling better control over unwanted habits or behaviors. The Brief Self-Control Scale allows users to assess their capacity for managing themselves. If improved upon, it can result in forming healthier alternatives instead of giving into bad habits like smoking or unhealthy snacking, for example.

Creating Supportive Environments:

Creating a supportive environment to promote positive social, academic, and emotional growth outcomes, cultivate good habits, and discourage negative ones is crucial. The Greatness app can be a valuable tool in this process, providing a platform to track progress, set clear expectations, and offer incentives for personal development. By utilizing the app's features, such as goal-setting and habit tracking, individuals can foster trust, communication, and a sense of security within their environment. With the support of the Greatness app, everyone can have faith in each other's abilities and access the necessary resources to thrive physically and emotionally in this nurturing space.

The psychology of habit plays a significant role in our everyday lives. Understanding how the habit loop works can help us control our habits, be they bad or good. We also discuss a few things that can impact bad habits and methods for breaking them.

There is advice about forming helpful patterns. Along with creating an encouraging atmosphere for yourself, being determined and dedicated goes a long way! It would be best to have discipline when taking charge of your behavior, as this will enable you to live the life you deserve without limitations set by poor practices.

4.5 Integrating Brain-Based Techniques for Lasting Change

"What we learn with pleasure, we never forget."
– Alfred Mercier

Have you observed that when you read something, you understand it, but teaching the same thing to others is a different experience?
What do you do?
You start by translating the information into your own words. This process alone helps solidify new knowledge in your brain. Next, find some way to share what you have learned. Some ideas include writing a blog post, creating a podcast, or participating in a group discussion.

Let us start by understanding what Brain-Based Learning is.

Brain-based learning is a paradigm that addresses student learning and learning outcomes from the perspective of the human brain. It involves specific learning strategies designed based on how human attention, memory, motivation, and conceptual knowledge acquisition work. This chapter will explore how brain-based learning and teaching can optimize learning holistically.

Historically, teaching and learning have been primarily based on what students, teachers, and policy-makers think. Their opinions, experiences, logical arguments, and quasi-experiments in the classroom inform the teaching and learning process. Brain-based learning takes a different approach. The way students are motivated, the way attention works, the way memories are formed, the way information is presented, etc., become the central aspects of teaching and learning.

One example is the ***construal level theory***, which can address when and how a student should focus on the minute details in learning materials. *Intuitively, one could say that* *details are essential for mastery, and students should learn details to demonstrate proficiency. However, this blanket statement is not an evidence-based approach. The construal level theory shows that understanding an overview without the details can engage a more extensive network of concepts a student learns or is sensitized to. Understanding the essence of a specific topic can also promote creativity because capturing the essence of a concept makes the concept vague and abstract. An abstract entity links to more abstract entities and makes the learning broad instead of details, making the learning narrow and specific.*

This was just one example of how a brain-based learning approach can better inform teaching and learning.

A brain-based approach does not necessarily include intelligence testing, aptitude testing, and other standardized tests. While these can sometimes yield helpful information, they are not required to utilize a brain-based approach. In some corner cases, it might be necessary – when there is significant cognitive impairment, physical disability, emotional distress due to confusion about careers, etc.

This approach can be considered quite accommodating because it does not discard valuable information or is evidence-based for superficial reasons like not falling into a particular perspective or pedagogy. [49]

1. Learn in Multiple ways:

Empower yourself by learning in more than one way. Instead of just listening to a podcast, which involves auditory learning, take the initiative to find a way to rehearse the information verbally and visually. This might involve describing what you learned from a friend, taking notes, or drawing a mind map.

You are memorizing and genuinely understanding and retaining the knowledge by learning in multiple ways. As Judy Willis puts it, *"The more regions of the brain that store data about a subject, the more interconnection there is. This redundancy means students will have more opportunities to pull up all related data bits from their multiple storage areas in response to a single cue. This cross-referencing of data means we have learned, rather than just memorized"* **(*Willis, J. Brain-based teaching strategies for improving students' memory, learning, and test-taking success. Review of Research. Childhood Education, 83(5), 31-316, 2008).***

2. Teach What you have learned from Another Person:

Educators have long noted that one of the best ways to learn something is to teach it to someone else. Remember your seventh-grade presentation on Costa Rica? By teaching to the rest of the class, your teacher hoped you would gain even more from the assignment. You can apply the same principle today by sharing your newly learned skills and knowledge with others. *Start by translating the information into your own words. This process alone helps solidify new knowledge in your brain. Next, find some way to share what you have learned. Some ideas include writing a blog post, creating a podcast, or participating in a group discussion.*

3. Utilize Previous Learning to Promote New Learning

Deepen your understanding and connection to the learning material by utilizing previous learning to promote new learning. Another great way to become more effective is to use relational learning, which involves relating new information to things you already know. *For example, suppose you are learning about Romeo and Juliet. In that case, you might associate what you learn about the play with prior knowledge about Shakespeare, the historical period in which the author lived, and other relevant information.*

4. Gain Practical Experience

For many of us, learning typically involves reading textbooks, attending lectures, or researching in the library or on the Web. While seeing information and writing it down is essential, putting new knowledge and skills into practice can be one of the best ways to improve learning. *If you are trying to acquire a new skill or ability, focus on gaining practical experience. If it is a sport or athletic skill, perform the activity regularly. If you are learning a new language, practice speaking with another person and surround yourself with immersive experiences.* If you see a standardized patient, observe a physician examining a patient, hear about a disease, take time to read about it. This helps you learn—by connecting to a natural person.

5. Look Up Answers Rather Than Struggle to Remember

Learning is a dynamic process, and forgetting some details is natural. Remember that research suggests a simple solution when you struggle to recall information: look up the correct answer. A study revealed that the longer you spend trying to remember, the more likely you will forget again. This is because these attempts to recall can lead to learning the 'error state' instead of the correct response. So, empower yourself by embracing the practicality of looking up answers.

6. Understand How You Learn Best

Enhancing learning efficiency is not a one-size-fits-all approach. It is about recognizing and embracing your unique learning habits and styles. Various theories, such as Gardner's Theory of multiple intelligences, can provide insights into your learning strengths. This personalized understanding can make you feel more understood and catered to in your learning journey.

7. Use Testing to Boost Learning

While it may seem that spending more time studying is one of the best ways to maximize learning, research has demonstrated that taking tests helps you better remember what you have learned, even if it was not covered on the test. The study revealed that students who studied and were tested had better long-term recall of the materials, even on information not covered by the tests. Students who had extra time to study but were not tested had significantly lower recall of the materials.

8. Stop Multitasking

For many years, it was thought that people who multitask or perform more than one activity at once had an edge over those who did not. However, research now suggests that multitasking can make learning less effective. In the study, participants lost significant amounts of time as they switched between multiple tasks and lost even more time as the tasks became increasingly complex. By switching from one activity to another, you will learn more slowly, become less efficient, and make more errors. How can you avoid the dangers of multitasking? Start by focusing on the task and working for a predetermined time.

4.6 10 Main Takeaways: Rewiring Your Brain: Unraveling the Neuroscience of Change

1. **Neuroplasticity and Mindset Shifts:** Understanding neuroplasticity allows individuals to reframe their thoughts and behaviors by actively rewiring their brains. Techniques such as relabeling negative thoughts, identifying their source, and refocusing attention positively can facilitate lasting behavioral changes.
2. **Practical Strategies for Enhancing Neuroplasticity**: Daily nutrition, adequate sleep, and mental exercises (e.g., using the non-dominant hand and learning new skills) can strengthen neural pathways and improve cognitive flexibility and performance.
3. **Impact of Dopamine and Serotonin**: Recognizing the roles of dopamine in motivation and serotonin in mood regulation underscores their importance in mental well-being. Balanced levels of these neurotransmitters through lifestyle adjustments can enhance happiness and productivity.
4. **Biological Basis of Happiness**: Happiness involves complex biological and environmental factors interplay. Genetic predispositions and brain chemistry significantly influence one's ability to experience and sustain happiness.

5. **Practical Applications in Daily Life:** Integrating mindfulness practices, maintaining a healthy lifestyle, and fostering positive social connections can optimize brain function, promote emotional resilience, and enhance overall life satisfaction.
6. **Understanding Habit Formation:** Habits are behaviors repeated regularly and subconsciously, influenced by cues and rewards. To develop good habits like exercise or healthier eating, simplify the process and make it enjoyable, such as exercising with a friend or prepping easy meals. Breaking bad habits involves identifying triggers and substituting them with healthier alternatives supported by a supportive environment.
7. **Challenges in Habit Development**: Initial effort, consistency, and the lure of instant gratification are common hurdles in forming good habits. Overambitious goals and a lack of patience can lead to setbacks. It is crucial to start small, practice early in the day, and repeat consistently to override brain resistance.
8. **Integrating Brain-Based Learning:** Brain-based learning enhances retention by engaging multiple senses and teaching others what you have learned. Relating new information to previous knowledge, gaining practical experience, and using testing to reinforce learning are effective strategies. Understanding your unique learning style and avoiding multitasking also promote effective learning.
9. **Practical Strategies for Lasting Change**: Recognize triggers for bad habits, gradually replace routines, and maintain progress by tracking behavior. Setting realistic

goals and understanding motivation are crucial to breaking bad habits and fostering good ones.

10. **Creating Supportive Environments:** Foster an environment conducive to positive habits by leveraging tools like habit-tracking apps and setting clear goals. Building a supportive social circle and cultivating willpower through mindfulness and self-control techniques enhance habit formation

Chapter 5: Vulnerability: The Gateway to Resilience and Authenticity

5.1 Redefining Vulnerability: Dispelling the Myth

"Vulnerability is the birthplace of innovation, creativity, and change."
– Brené Brown

How Starbucks CEO Howard Schultz Inspired Us to Dream Bigger:

On a cold January day in 1961, **Fred Schultz**, ***a diaper delivery serviceman***, fell on a sheet of ice and broke his hip and his ankle. Fred's son, **Howard**, was seven years old and vividly remembers the accident. ***"That image of my father, slumped on the family couch, his leg in a cast, unable to work or earn money, and ground down by the world is still burned into my mind,"*** the **Starbucks CEO** once said. At the time of the accident, the Schultz family was living in a Brooklyn housing project. They had no health insurance, worker's comp, severance, or way to make ends meet. Young Howard vowed that if he were ever in a position to care for people, he would strive to make a difference in their lives.

The story is the foundation for nearly every initiative Starbucks implemented under Schultz's leadership: health benefits for part-time workers, tuition assistance, veterans hiring, and an employee stock purchase program.

"Starbucks has become a living legacy of my dad," he said.

Although Schultz, a self-made billionaire, has announced that he will step away as CEO of Starbucks beginning April 3, 2017, I have no doubt we will hear about Schultz's ***'origin story'*** time and time again in whatever role Schultz pursues. Schultz is proud of his roots because, as he once said, ***"The more uninspiring your origins, the more likely you are to use your imagination and invent worlds where everything seems possible."***

"Coffee is what we sell as a product, but it is not our business. We are in the people business," Schultz responded. "I am passionate about human connection."

Schultz often says:

Passion is everything.

A leader cannot inspire without it.

"When you are surrounded by people who share a passionate commitment around a common purpose, anything is possible," Schultz told me.

Here is how Schultz recalled the experience in an interview with Oprah Winfrey:

"People think I am the founder of Starbucks. I was an employee when Starbucks only had four stores. I was sent to Italy on a trip to Starbucks and returned feeling that the Starbucks business was wrong. I wanted to bring back the daily ritual, the sense of community, and the idea that we could build this third place between home and work in America. It was an epiphany. I was out of my mind. I walked in

and saw this symphony of activity, the romance, and the theater of coffee. Moreover, coffee is the center of the conversation, creating a sense of community. That is what spoke to me."

Five significant leadership lessons from Howard Schultz:

- Inspiring leaders are not as passionate about the products their companies make as they are about how the products or services improve the lives of their employees and customers.
- Inspiring leaders never grow tired of sharing stories that shaped their character.
- Inspiring leaders treat employees benevolently.
- Inspiring leaders obsess over every aspect of the customer experience.
- Inspiring leaders remind themselves—and their employees—of what business they are in.

Above all, Howard Schultz ignites our inner fire by embracing and sharing his story of triumph over adversity. By doing so, he teaches all of us—leaders, managers, entrepreneurs, and students—to dream big dreams and not to be afraid of chasing moonshots.[50]

According to **Brene Brown's *Netflix Special, The Call to Courage***. It is an exceptional piece of thought leadership that you cannot remain the same after watching.

Have you ever heard the word ***vulnerability*** and ***cringed***, associating the word with weakness or with a specific type of individual?

Most of us grew up hearing our parents say, ***'Be brave,'*** followed by ***'Do not cry.'***

Our parents did not understand that bravery is not holding it all in; bravery is pushing through discomfort to let it out and be seen.

Contrary to popular belief, courage, and vulnerability are not on opposite ends of the spectrum. Courage and vulnerability are the same. According to **Brene Brown**, vulnerability involves three things. Those three things are:

1. ***Uncertainty***
2. ***Risk***
3. ***Emotional exposure.***

She asks if you can think of one example of courage that did not require uncertainty, risk, or emotional exposure.

Crickets........

You can't because it does not exist. You cannot be courageous in words or actions without taking a risk, exposing yourself emotionally, or being uncertain of the outcome. Being silent keeps you safe and small, hidden from sight. Brave leaders are never silent around tough things.

The 5 Myths About Vulnerability:

1. ***Vulnerability is not Weakness.***

Vulnerability takes great strength to push through the discomfort and the unknown. It is easy to do things when we can control the outcome. It is not so easy when we cannot.

2. I do not do Vulnerability.

So, either you do vulnerability, or it does you. You either

do it consciously or unknowingly. It is much easier for us to cause pain than it is to feel pain. When you do not acknowledge your vulnerability, you take your shit out on other people. STOP taking your shit out on other people.

3. We Cannot Go It Alone.

We are neurobiologically hard-wired to connect with others. Without connection, love, and belonging, there is always suffering.

4. You Cannot Engineer the Discomfort Out of Vulnerability.

The minute it becomes comfortable, it is not vulnerable.

5. Trust Comes Before Vulnerability.

Vulnerability minus boundaries is not vulnerability. Brene goes on to explain, for example, that live tweeting your bikini wax is not an example of vulnerability. Posting on Facebook about your divorce, which your kids and colleagues can see, is not vulnerability. You measure vulnerability not by the amount of disclosure but by the courage to show up and be seen when you cannot control the outcome. (read that again)

What I know for sure is this... If we want a fantastic relationship, the promotion of our dream job, freedom in our hearts, and the fulfillment of human connection, we must have the courage to show up and be seen. To know that we are going to get our asses kicked more than once, and it is going to suck. Moreover, to trust that even though it does suck, being in the arena, being authentic, and playing BIG (not small) will allow us to feel the beautiful things that we only get to experience with courage.

Have the courage to show up and be seen today. You are worth it. [51]

5.2 Leveraging Vulnerability for Personal Growth: Stepping into Discomfort

"I wish you ample doses of pain and suffering."

That is the unconventional message **Nvidia CEO** and founder **Jensen Huang** had for students at Stanford University, his alma mater, where he spoke last month at the Stanford Institute for Economic Policy Research.
According to **Huang**, ***"Elite educational pedigrees alone are not necessarily the best predictor of success."***
"Greatness is not intelligence. Greatness comes from character. Moreover, the character is not formed out of smart people but out of people who suffered," said the Stanford alum.
Instead, the man who presides over one of the world's most valuable companies in stock market valuation now looks for specific traits in job applicants, including resilience, grit, and determination, which he contends lead to innovation and success in the workplace.
Counterintuitively, **Huang** believes that ***having high expectations from an Ivy League education can potentially set people up for less resilience when***

faced with failure or adversity, which are inevitable in any career path.

"Unfortunately, resilience matters in success," he told the students. ***"I do not know how to teach it to you except for I hope suffering happens to you."***

His comments indicate a view that real-world experience involving struggles, obstacles, and suffering can instill the resilience needed for long-term success. Therefore, he believes that employers should look beyond just the prestige factor of a university and more closely at potential hires' inner drive, mindset, and resolution.

"To this day, I use the phrase 'pain and suffering' inside our company with great glee," said the chief executive. ***"I mean that happily because you want to refine the character of your company. You want greatness out of them."***

In 2011, Huang shared a similar sentiment in another speech he gave at Stanford, stating, ***"Unless you have a tolerance for failure, you will never experiment, and if you do not ever experiment, you will never innovate. If you do not innovate, you fail."***

Hiring PHDs

The Nvidia founder's statements about valuing resilience over educational pedigrees align with the old Wall Street adage about hiring what they call "**PHD**s"—the ***poor***, ***hungry***, and ***driven***.

The core parallels are prioritizing ***hunger***, ***grit***, and ***motivation*** over academic credentials alone and believing that candidates who have overcome adversity, financial hardships, or personal trauma offer invaluable drive and tenacity. Both schools of thought find real-world fight and scrappiness desirable, in addition to raw intellectual ability. These philosophies prioritize the intangibles. Skepticism exists that those who come from privileged backgrounds lack ***"hunger"*** and may be less resilient and more entitled.

The **PHD** concept argues that if handled constructively, struggle can be an excellent preparation for thriving in ultra-competitive business environments where stamina and an insatiable work ethic are keys to success.

The idea is to harness difficult experiences as motivation for growth. With the right mindset, life's challenges can forge competent professionals. Resilience, enduring trauma and difficulties, and mental toughness build mental toughness.

A person who had to fight for opportunities may have a stronger inner drive and motivation to succeed than those for whom things came quickly. This hunger can translate to a work ethic. Facing adversity often provides more profound empathy and understanding of the struggles others face, which can build better emotional intelligence and people skills.

Overcoming adversity requires adaptability and comfort with ambiguity. These mindsets are very valuable in ever-changing work environments. Wrestling with significant life challenges can provide a sense of perspective often lacking in those with smoother paths. This can sharpen priorities and decision-making.

Hiring managers want to see applicants who show resilience by acknowledging mistakes and reflecting on how to improve in the future. Individuals who self-reflect on what went wrong and have a clear plan for what to do differently later are determined to persist in past mistakes. This quality highlights their ability to adapt and learn from failures, essential traits for grit. [52]

Embracing Vulnerability: The Key to Authenticity and Personal Growth:

In our quest for perfection, we often hide our flaws and shun our weaknesses, forgetting that fragility and vulnerability are intrinsic human parts.

How often do we find ourselves putting on a brave face, concealing our fears and insecurities?

By doing so, we fail to realize the power of vulnerability and how it can foster authenticity and personal growth.

In this journey, we will explore the intriguing nature of vulnerability, debunk some common misconceptions about it, and decipher its significant role in fostering authenticity. We will scrutinize the transformative impact vulnerability can have on our growth journey. Finally, we will delve into some actionable and experienced steps to embrace vulnerability.

So, let us dive in, embrace our vulnerability, and open the door to a more authentic and fulfilling life. The road to personal growth starts here. Embrace the ride!

Vulnerability and Authenticity:

In the hustle and bustle of modern life, we often hide behind masks, seldom revealing our authentic selves. However, we cannot overlook the profound connection between vulnerability and authenticity. *When we step into our vulnerability, we begin a journey toward authenticity, a path that promises self-discovery and genuine fulfillment.*

How Vulnerability Leads to Authenticity:

Vulnerability is not about weakness; it is about openness. It is the courage to expose our weaknesses, hopes, and fears in all their rawness, with the conviction that this honesty will lead us closer to our authentic selves.

Consider these reasons why vulnerability can be seen as a pathway to authenticity:

Foster Trust: When we open up about our vulnerabilities, we show people we are human, just like them. This shared humanity creates a bond of trust, allowing for deeper and more genuine connections.

Promote Self-Love: Embracing our vulnerabilities helps us stop pretending and accept ourselves. This shifts our mindset from self-criticism to self-love, leading to authenticity.

Encourage Growth: Opening ourselves to vulnerability enables us to confront our weaknesses. This promotes self-improvement and personal growth, pushing us towards becoming the best versions of ourselves.

The Role of Vulnerability in Self-discovery:

One of the great truths I have learned is that vulnerability is crucial in uncovering our authentic selves and an essential ingredient in self-discovery. This journey, while often demanding and challenging, is also noticeably transformative.

Here is its essence in these critical points:

Gain Insight: By acknowledging our vulnerabilities, we gain insight into our strengths and weaknesses, desires, and fears. This understanding provides a clear lens through which to view our authentic selves.

Develop Emotional Intelligence: Vulnerability helps us connect with our feelings. We learn to identify, understand, and manage our emotions better, cultivating emotional intelligence, a critical aspect of self-discovery.

Experience Freedom: Being vulnerable frees us from the burden of facades. We are no longer tied down by the exhausting endeavor of keeping up appearances, allowing us to relax into our true selves.

By daring to be vulnerable, we liberate ourselves to journey toward authenticity. So, let us not shy away from vulnerability but embrace it, for we discover our most authentic selves in these honest and genuine moments. Trust me, vulnerability is not as scary as it seems, and the rewards—authenticity, self-discovery, and personal growth—are priceless.

Vulnerability's Impact on Personal Growth:

Unlike what most people believe, vulnerability is not a disadvantage; it is a potent catalyst for personal growth. Grappling with vulnerability empowers us to embrace challenges and accept our authentic selves – unlocking boundless potential for advancement and fulfillment.

Embracing Challenges:

Every person has faced situations at some point in their life where they expose their innermost fears, doubts, and perceived inadequacies to themselves or others. This exposure is the root of vulnerability. However, instead of considering it a handicap, we must shift our perception and see vulnerability as an opportunity for self-improvement.

Overcoming fears: Confronting our fears is a significant aspect of embracing vulnerability. Instead of retreating into our comfort zones when we face these fears, stepping up and facing them head-on helps us to grow.

Building resilience: Next, vulnerability builds resilience. With every difficulty we face, we become more robust and adaptive. This strength is crucial in personal and professional life, making us rise against adversity.

Improving problem-solving skills: Finally, vulnerability enhances our problem-solving skills. When we start exploring our weaknesses, we also uncover ways to turn them into assets, increasing our ability to handle different issues.

"Vulnerability is not winning or losing; it is having the courage to show up and be seen when we have no control over the outcome."
– Brene Brown.

Growth through Acceptance:

Accepting our vulnerability does not mean succumbing to it. Instead, it honors our humanity, making us more compassionate and empathetic.

Here is why:

Boosts self-awareness: Acknowledging our vulnerabilities and shortcomings heightens our self-awareness. We learn about our strengths and areas for development, making us more confident individuals.

Enhances emotional intelligence: Vulnerability can also boost our emotional intelligence. It helps us better understand and control our emotions, which can significantly improve our interactions and relationships with others.

Promotes authenticity: By embracing our vulnerabilities, we allow ourselves to be genuinely who we are without any social mask. This authenticity makes us more approachable and relatable.

Understanding our vulnerabilities may be daunting, but it is a brave journey that liberates us from our chains of insecurity. This expanse of understanding gives birth to an unshakeable self-belief, inevitably leading to extraordinary personal growth.

So, let us celebrate the beauty of vulnerability; it is the beacon guiding us toward genuine enlightenment and personal development. After all, growth and comfort do not coexist. We must step out of our comfort zones and proudly wear our vulnerabilities to grow.

How to Embrace Vulnerability?

Embracing vulnerability can be a significant challenge but also an empowering endeavor. While it may seem daunting initially, opening up about your emotions and admitting your fears and insecurities is one of the most potent catalysts for personal growth and deeper connections. It is all about finding balance and understanding that being vulnerable does not mean you are weak, but rather, you are authentic. Let us embrace vulnerability by acknowledging fears and uncertainties, practicing self-compassion, and living mindfully.

Acknowledging Fear and Uncertainties

Recognizing your fears and uncertainties can be crucial in embracing vulnerability. We all have them; they are part of the human condition. You may fear rejection, failure, or even success.

Take time to identify what you are afraid of.

Write them down: This helps acknowledge that these fears exist.

Understand that everyone has insecurities: you are not alone in this.

Remember, bravery is not about having no fears but facing them. Thus, acknowledging your worries and uncertainties can lead to great strides in accepting vulnerability.

Practicing Self-Compassion:

Practicing self-compassion is another fantastic way to start embracing vulnerability. When we are kind to ourselves, we provide a safe space for vulnerability to thrive.

Here are a few ways you can cultivate self-compassion:

Be patient with yourself: Personal growth takes time.

Acknowledge your effort, not just the outcome.

Remind yourself that everyone has flaws and makes mistakes.

"Talk to yourself like you would to someone you love" is a statement rooted in self-compassion. It is about understanding that you deserve kindness and care despite your flaws and mistakes.

Mindful Living and Vulnerability

Finally, living mindfully can be remarkably beneficial in learning to embrace vulnerability. Mindfulness, the practice of being fully present and engaged at the moment, allows us to experience our feelings without judgment. This awareness allows us to be honest and open without fearing how our emotions may be perceived.

To practice mindfulness:

Slow down and embrace the present.
Notice and accept your feelings without judgment.
Practice breathing exercises or mindfulness meditation.
Indeed, meditation is essential for promoting mindfulness; this comprehensive guide, Mindfulness Meditation Guide, explains its benefits in more detail.

All in all, embracing vulnerability is not a one-size-fits-all process. It is a continuous journey of acknowledging fears, practicing self-compassion, and living mindfully. When you are vulnerable, you open the door to profound personal growth and connections with others. It is not easy, but the rewards are worth the effort.[53]

5.3 Vulnerability in Relationships: Navigating Conflict

"Of course, I will hurt you. Of course, you will hurt me. Of course, we will hurt each other. However, this is the very condition of existence. To become spring means accepting the risk of winter. To become present means accepting the risk of absence."

-Antoine de Saint-Exupery

In 2016, I saw a couple dancing to the tune of folk songs from Goa, India, for the first time on a cruise, and we, along with a few friends and the children, enjoyed the ride. They were in typical Goan costume. The top deck was fully crowded, and they stared at each other passionately, their facial expressions a parody of romantic jealousy. The performance was marked with elaborate and dramatic movements which exaggerated the sultry, fiery tone. We completed our joyride and walked away from it, not feeling particularly moved until I dived deep into the subject of vulnerability while writing this book.

What I captured had not been feigned for onlookers. I remember two photos that showed the intimacy of their close embrace as the dancers closed their eyes and clung to each other. In the moments when they were not pretending for tourists, their yearning for connection was expressed through the tightness of their union in between flips and tricks. I still have those photos to remind me that vulnerability makes us beautiful, human, and authentic. Expressing it genuinely brings us closer to others, builds trust, and allows us to experience life with all our hearts and emotions.

That is not an easy conclusion; for many of us, it is something we must re-learn. As children, we were told not to reveal too much of ourselves because our communities might not accept it.

I feel sad for men who cannot even get in touch with their emotions, let alone express them, because they were taught this was weak, and somehow, it equated to being feminine. Women also find it hard to appear imperfect. We are judged daily on what we wear, what we say, how we behave, and whether we ask for it.

Every relationship starts with a dream full of promises that have been nurtured over the years:

What happens after some time?
Why did distance start to increase between the spouses?
Why is there so much intolerance between them?
Gradually, why does it lead to many miseries, including separation?
What makes the U-turn impossible?
Why do most people live in under-average relationships?
Most people start to feel lonely very soon.
Most people start to miss their old life and friends.

What are some common reasons for relationships ending despite a robust initial connection?

Because their partner puts effort into the beginning, once they stop putting in the effort, the other cannot continue putting in the effort unless they see the effort being put in for them.

Here are some common factors that make this happen.

1. As time passes, one realizes the goals are entirely different. Your partner may want an entire adventurous life, while you may want to be sitting at home sipping a cup of coffee

2. As time passes, your priorities on how you want to live with your partner and make memories more important than just that love talk

3. As time passes, it becomes real every day. You start feeling FOMO (Fear Of Missing Out)seeing other partners enjoying while you feel like missing out on adventures you had thought to have with your partner, so you become restless

4. As time passes, your partner or even you become so comfortable that you take each other for granted and feel like an essential love or romantic gesture is a lot of 'work.' While one may not be much affected by it, the other may completely feel devoid of love and attention

5. As time passes, family comes into play. Your partner may feel uneasy with the family intrusions, especially negative ones. One partner may always be unaffected

6. As time passes, future conversations become essential. One partner may start to feel that you spent a great deal of time waiting for the beautiful memories but cannot afford to wait anymore, so they start pressuring the other partner for plans in the future so they do not regret anymore

7. As time passes, intimacy is also taken for granted. One partner starts to feel negligent of how much it is to keep the bond while the other may feel disconnected, not seeing any efforts to feel loved

8. As time passes, one partner starts to give more time and priority to one's freedom and time and hobbies while the other partner gets confused and feels ignored for the beginning of the relationship, both did most of the things together

Why?

In relationships, our choices and actions can be driven by two fundamental emotions: love and fear. At the same time, fear may seem like a natural response to protect ourselves, but operating from a place of love can transform our relationships. By consciously choosing love over fear, we can nurture healthy connections, foster growth, and create a harmonious environment for love to flourish. This article will explore the significance of operating from love over fear in relationships and how it can positively shape our interactions. [54]

Brene Brown, a leading shame researcher, found that we all

feel shame, and if you do not, it is because you have no capacity for human emotion. We experience shame as a fear of disconnection from others, that we will not be accepted if we reveal who we are to them. In extreme cases, people who experience abuse do not even talk about their trauma because they feel so unworthy of love and acceptance that they must hide their experience, even from themselves.

You might need to hide a mistake at work because if people knew about it, they may no longer accept you as a highly educated professional. You may feel that people would see you as weak if you told them that you have a mental illness or that you are grieving somebody you love, which is why you are finding it hard to perform at your usual levels. Shame shows up in all sorts of ways, but the essential feature of it is an unwillingness to be who you are because others may reject that part of you. That is a painful, isolating, and unhappy place to be. [55]

Wholeheartedness:

We have learned to numb our vulnerabilities through drinking, drugs, eating, pretending, and a whole raft of other ways that stop us from facing the discomfort of being imperfect. I do not even know what it means to be perfect!

The problem is that you cannot just numb one emotion; you must numb everything, including joy, love, happiness, and satisfaction. Our humanity resides in allowing and being open to our vulnerabilities, observing them, and compassionate toward them.

When you live wholeheartedly, you take risks. You accept that asking out somebody might lead to rejection, but you do it anyway. You know that if you quit a job that makes you unhappy, things might not work out, but that is ok. Failure is not something to be ashamed of.

You understand that when you express your deepest secret to a friend, they might be disappointed in you, but that does not change your approval of yourself.

You know you are worthy despite your imperfections and flaws. You know nobody can reject you because you accept yourself. People who have this inner belief are not judgmental of others. Instead, they see the beauty in vulnerability and know that it is a necessary part of being alive. It does not mean it is easy to sit with, but the alternative is emotional emptiness. We stop feeling ashamed of appearing stupid, failing, not being attractive enough, not being whatever enough. We are satisfied with whatever there is.

What Does This Mean for Conflict?

While training to become a lawyer, I learned to find ways to blame the other party. Lawyers are paid to analyze the rules, laws, and procedures and to develop positions and defenses to convince a judge that they are right and the other party is wrong. The aim is to control the outcome; the more concrete your position is, the better. These positions can become so entrenched that parties can spend thousands of pounds proving that they are right.

I am not saying that legal action is inappropriate in some situations, but you should be aware of your vulnerabilities and look at them realistically. Pretending you have none is costly in a natural, practical sense.

It is doubtful that you are one hundred percent right in any conflict. Conflict is complex and is usually accompanied by high emotions, new and old wounds, and interests and needs that are left wanting. This can lead to you fighting something you will lose in more ways than one.

People who do not accept or express their vulnerabilities are most likely to blame somebody else and insist on being right. They build walls around themselves during conflict and throw stones at the other party. That is what blame is: a defense mechanism that discharges pain and suffering onto the other person. It comes from shame.

Conflict and Vulnerability:

When parties to a conflict perceive that they will "win," they usually do not want to negotiate or resolve the conflict in another way. They believe they are correct, often fueled by lawyers, friends, relatives, or anything supporting that position.

We do not tend to recognize our vulnerabilities until something happens, which makes us realize that we will not win and that the conflict hurts us more than we can stand. When the other party has the same perception, this usually results in attempts to resolve conflict.

Parties then reason that the costs of pursuing a legal battle outweigh the claim amount. This can be persuasive in bringing parties together.

In interpersonal disputes, parties might feel emotionally exhausted, or after a period of absence from the other party, they may realize their relationship is worth saving.

Resolving Conflict Using Wholeheartedness:

In order to be vulnerable, you need to be honest about your feelings, needs, and, crucially, what you want from a resolution.

Starting any conversation by acknowledging how you feel and

how the other person seems to feel and committing to moving forward with a conflict will, at the very least, get the other party's attention.

Telling them that both of you are negatively affected by the conflict may get them to think seriously about resolving it. [56] It might not; you might be rejected. They may ignore you and carry on as before. Nonetheless, this will provide you with valuable information. The conflict is not ripe yet for resolution. Maybe the other party's perception of the conflict differs from yours. The answer may be to wait until emotions and perceptions have died down.

You can be sure that approaching conflict with a willingness to admit to mistakes, apologize if you cause harm, and openly understand the other person's interests, needs, and emotions will help you contain conflict and come to mutually beneficial solutions. You will feel empowered and may even find a renewed, more profound connection with somebody you once despised.

I say none of this is easy. My emotions are still a battle, and I often have to give myself a pep talk about how I react to somebody. I always have to step back from my emotions and take time out to let them self-expire before I read over what I have written and attempt to put it into practice. The fact that you are reading this blog post is a step in the right direction, for which you should give yourself credit.

According to renowned researcher Brene Brown and her groundbreaking concept of the "power of vulnerability," vulnerability in relationships can be defined as the willingness to open oneself up emotionally, share one's thoughts and feelings honestly, and express genuine authenticity without fear of judgment or rejection.

Acceptance Versus Judgment:

Choosing acceptance over judgment changes a relationship's entire vibe and dynamic. Fear often leads to judgment and criticism, creating a divide between partners. Operating from love means choosing acceptance. Instead of focusing on flaws or shortcomings, we embrace our partners for who they are, celebrating their strengths and accepting their imperfections. By choosing acceptance, we create an atmosphere of unconditional love and support, encouraging personal growth and self-expression. This fosters an environment where both partners feel safe to be authentic, enhancing the connection and creating a solid foundation for a healthy relationship.

Fear Is Limiting

Fear can hinder effective communication, leading to misunderstandings and conflicts. However, we prioritize open and honest communication when we operate from love. We approach conversations with kindness, active listening, and a genuine desire to resolve issues and grow together. Operating from love encourages collaborative problem-solving, where both partners actively contribute to finding solutions. This fosters a sense of teamwork and mutual support, creating a strong and resilient bond.

Fear often limits our growth and keeps us in our comfort zones. Operating from love means embracing a growth mindset. We encourage personal and relationship growth, supporting each other's aspirations and celebrating achievements. By operating from love, we view challenges as opportunities for learning and transformation rather than threats. This mindset promotes continuous personal development and fosters a relationship dynamic where both partners feel empowered to pursue their dreams and evolve together.

Operating from love over fear is a conscious choice that can profoundly shape our relationships. We create an environment where love can thrive by embracing vulnerability, cultivating empathy and compassion, choosing acceptance, nurturing communication and collaboration, and cultivating a growth mindset. Remember, we build strong connections through love, foster personal and relationship growth, and create fulfilling and lasting partnerships. Choose love over fear, and watch as your relationships blossom and flourish. [57]

To have a close and robust relationship, emotional vulnerability is a must. I will explain below. To get the most satisfying and loving relationship requires us to be vulnerable in 4 domains:

Intellectual

Emotional

Spiritual

Physical

When two people know each other in all of these domains, we build closeness, trust, and a bond. The more you share and receive with your head, heart, spirit, and body in this order of priority, the more connected you become.

Emotional vulnerability is so critical because EMOTIONS ARE THE GREAT CONNECTORS. Remember this principle! Emotions connect our thoughts to the body and connect me with another person. Through noticing and sharing our emotions, we know ourselves and let others know us. Since emotions express the content of our intentions, thoughts, dreams, desires, and fears, it becomes possible to connect deeply with another person when you share these at the appropriate stage in your relationship.

When you do not share emotions, the other person will have gaps in their knowledge of you and naturally be inclined to create a narrative to fill in the story and guess your intentions, why you do what you do, and who you are. This often causes confusion, hurt, and a lack of trust. If someone does not know what you are feeling/thinking, how can they trust what they do not know?

Knowledge creates trust, but hidden emotions and thoughts create doubt and mistrust. There is no doubt about it; it is a risk to share your emotions, but that is how love works. Love is a risk. One can risk sharing deeply and possibly get hurt and rejected or loved, or not take the risk of sharing emotions and remaining lonely and disconnected. My bet is on risking love because it makes life meaningful and rich. Take a chance on love and share your heart. [58]

Golden point to be born in mind:

In daily life, the concepts of Mr. Right and Ms. Right are also idealizations, just like the concept of a reversible (perfect) process. People who insist on finding Mr. Right or Ms. Right to settle down are bound to remain Mr. or Ms. Single for the rest of their lives. The possibility of finding the perfect prospective mate is no higher than the possibility of finding a perfect 9reversible) process. Likewise, a person who insists on perfection in friendship is bound to have no friends. ***(Source: Thermodynamics: An Engineering Approach, by Congel and Boles)***

5.4 Vulnerability in Leadership: Leading with Authenticity

"Leadership is not about being in charge.
It is about taking care of those in your charge."
– Simon Sinek

From "know-it-alls" to "learn-it-all":

Soon after **Satya Nadella** became **CEO of Microsoft** in 2014, he set about transforming the tech giant's culture. His goal: Change from a place where people acted like ***"know-it-alls"***—unsurprising perhaps because the company had been dominant for so long—to a ***"learn-it-all"*** culture that is "about learning, listening, and harnessing individual passions and talents to the company's mission," as he writes in his 2017 book, Hit Refresh.

Few can dispute the impact of Microsoft's shift to a learn-it-all culture.

Nadella killed failing projects, such as a mobile phone operating system, and embraced promising opportunities like cloud computing. He has overseen a partnership with OpenAI, making Microsoft a leader in artificial intelligence. The company is currently the most valuable in the world, with a market capitalization north of $3 trillion.

When Nadella took over at Microsoft, the company struggled to keep up with its tech industry competitors. Nadella knew that he needed to make significant changes to turn things around but also knew he could not do it alone.

So, instead of projecting an image of infallibility, Nadella was open about his doubts and insecurities – he embraced vulnerability as a leader. He admitted that he did not have all the answers and needed his team's help to achieve their goals. He encouraged his employees to speak up and share their ideas and opinions, even if they disagreed with him.

This vulnerability paid off in spades. Under Nadella's leadership, Microsoft has become one of the world's most successful and innovative companies. *By creating an environment of trust and openness, Nadella has inspired his employees to be more creative and productive and has fostered a culture of innovation that has driven Microsoft's success.*

The importance of vulnerability in leadership cannot be overstated. Leaders can create an atmosphere of trust and collaboration essential for success by being open and honest about their limitations and weaknesses. Moreover, by embracing vulnerability as a leadership trait, they can inspire their teams to achieve great things and drive the organization to new heights of success. [59]

Vulnerability and Leadership:

Leadership is often associated with qualities like strength, confidence, and decisiveness. However, one trait that is increasingly recognized as essential for effective leadership is vulnerability.

Contrary to popular belief, vulnerability in leadership does not signify weakness but rather the courage to be authentic, open, and transparent.

This sub-chapter will explore the concept of vulnerability in leadership and its profound impact on creating psychological safety within teams and fostering workplace innovation.

By embracing vulnerability, leaders can create an environment where team members feel safe to take risks, share ideas, and collaborate, leading to increased creativity, engagement, and organizational success. Let us delve into the power of vulnerability in leadership and its role in cultivating psychological safety and driving workplace innovation.

Defining Vulnerability in Leadership

Vulnerability in leadership refers to the willingness of leaders to show their authentic selves, admit their limitations, and openly express their thoughts and emotions. It involves being genuine and transparent, allowing others to see a leader's strengths and vulnerabilities. Rather than projecting an image of invincibility, vulnerable leaders acknowledge their imperfections and demonstrate humility. *By embracing vulnerability, leaders create an atmosphere of trust and authenticity within their teams.*

Authenticity is a cornerstone of vulnerability in leadership. When leaders are authentic, they establish a genuine connection with their team members, fostering an environment where individuals feel comfortable being themselves. This authenticity builds trust, as team members recognize that their leaders are approachable, understanding, and empathetic.

Lead by example:

By embracing vulnerability and authenticity, leaders demonstrate that it is safe for team members to share their ideas, opinions, and concerns. This, in turn, fosters a culture of trust and psychological safety where individuals feel valued, supported, and respected. When team members trust their leaders, they are more likely to take risks, offer innovative solutions, and collaborate effectively, increasing productivity and creativity.

In summary, vulnerability in leadership involves being authentic, transparent, and willing to acknowledge one's vulnerabilities. By building trust and creating an atmosphere of psychological safety, vulnerable leaders empower their teams to bring their best selves to work, contributing to a culture of innovation and success.

The Role of Vulnerability in Creating Psychological Safety:

Vulnerability plays a crucial role in creating psychological safety within teams and organizations. When leaders demonstrate vulnerability, they contribute to the establishment of an environment where individuals feel safe taking risks, expressing their opinions, and engaging in open communication without fear of judgment or negative consequences.

Leaders break down barriers and promote trust among team members by showing vulnerability. When leaders are open about challenges, insecurities, and mistakes, they humanize themselves and become relatable. This transparency creates a sense of trust and authenticity within the team, encouraging team members to be more open and vulnerable.

When team members see their leaders embracing vulnerability, they feel more comfortable sharing their ideas, concerns, and perspectives. This open communication leads to better team collaboration, problem-solving, and innovation. It fosters an environment where everyone's voice is valued and diverse viewpoints are welcomed.

Furthermore, vulnerability in leadership creates psychological safety by dispelling the fear of failure or making mistakes. When leaders openly admit their vulnerabilities and encourage a learning-oriented mindset, team members feel safe taking risks, experimenting, and learning from failures. This cultivates a culture of continuous improvement and growth, where individuals are unafraid to step outside their comfort zones and contribute their best.

Therefore, vulnerability in leadership is instrumental in creating psychological safety. By fostering trust, encouraging open communication, and embracing a learning-oriented mindset, leaders lay the foundation for a supportive and inclusive environment where individuals can thrive and achieve their full potential.

Building Trust through Vulnerability

Trust is a cornerstone of effective leadership and a cohesive work environment. One powerful way to build trust is through vulnerability. When leaders demonstrate vulnerability, they create a safe space for open communication, foster empathy, and strengthen relationships among team members.

Vulnerability in leadership involves being open and transparent about personal experiences, challenges, and emotions. By sharing their vulnerabilities, leaders show their authenticity and create a sense of relatability with their team members. This authenticity builds trust as team members see their leaders as genuine and trustworthy.

When leaders are vulnerable, they encourage others to reciprocate and share their thoughts, ideas, and concerns. This open exchange of vulnerabilities leads to deeper connections and understanding among team members. It also fosters empathy, as individuals can relate to and support one another based on shared experiences or challenges.

Moreover, vulnerability in leadership allows for mistakes and learning opportunities. When leaders acknowledge their shortcomings or mistakes, it creates an environment where team members feel safe to take risks and learn from their failures. This promotes a culture of growth and continuous improvement, strengthening trust in the process.

By embracing vulnerability, leaders demonstrate their trust in their team members. This trust encourages team members to be more authentic, take initiative, and contribute their best efforts. As trust grows, collaboration and teamwork become more effective, leading to higher levels of productivity and a more cohesive work environment.

Therefore, vulnerability in leadership is a powerful tool for building trust. Through openness, transparency, and empathy, leaders create an environment where team members feel safe to share their thoughts and concerns. This fosters more robust relationships, encourages collaboration, and leads to a more cohesive and successful work environment.

Fostering Innovation and Growth

Vulnerability in leadership builds trust and strengthens relationships and plays a crucial role in fostering innovation and driving growth within organizations. Leaders who exhibit vulnerability by creating a culture encouraging risk-taking, learning, and embracing new ideas set the stage for innovation to thrive.

When leaders demonstrate vulnerability, they create an environment where team members feel safe taking risks and thinking outside the box. By sharing their uncertainties and embracing the possibility of failure, leaders inspire their teams to push boundaries and explore innovative solutions. This mindset shift encourages creativity and the generation of new ideas, leading to breakthrough innovations.

Furthermore, vulnerability in leadership promotes a learning culture. When leaders openly acknowledge their areas for growth and embrace feedback, it sets an example for continuous learning and improvement. This mindset trickles down to team members, creating a culture that values personal and professional development. In such an environment, individuals are more willing to experiment, learn from their mistakes, and iterate on their ideas, fueling innovation and driving growth.

In addition, vulnerability encourages diverse perspectives and contributions. When leaders are open to different ideas and actively seek input from their team members, it fosters inclusivity and diversity of thought. Leaders can tap into their teams' collective intelligence and leverage diverse perspectives to drive innovation and growth by creating space for all voices to be heard.

By embracing vulnerability, leaders empower their teams to think innovatively, take calculated risks, and continuously learn and improve. This fosters a culture of innovation and growth, where new ideas are embraced, and individuals are motivated to push the boundaries of what is possible. Ultimately, organizations that prioritize vulnerability in leadership are better positioned to drive innovation, adapt to change, and achieve sustainable growth.

Overcoming Challenges and Resistance

While vulnerability in leadership has numerous benefits, it is not without its challenges and resistance. Leaders who aim to embrace vulnerability may encounter various obstacles along the way. However, these challenges can be overcome with the right strategies, allowing vulnerability to thrive.

One common challenge is the fear of judgment and criticism.

Leaders may hesitate to be vulnerable because they worry about how their team members or superiors will perceive them. Overcoming this challenge requires cultivating a supportive and nonjudgmental work environment where individuals feel safe sharing their vulnerabilities without fear of negative consequences. Creating a culture that values authenticity and emphasizes learning from mistakes can help alleviate this fear and encourage openness.

Resistance from team members is another challenge that leaders may face when practicing vulnerability. Some individuals may be uncomfortable with vulnerability and view it as a sign of weakness. To address this resistance, leaders can educate their teams about the benefits of vulnerability, highlighting how it fosters trust, encourages collaboration, and leads to better outcomes. Leaders can gradually inspire their team members to embrace vulnerability by setting an example and consistently demonstrating vulnerability.

Building resilience is also crucial when facing challenges and resistance. Leaders need to develop their resilience to overcome setbacks and persevere in their commitment to vulnerability. This includes cultivating a growth mindset, seeking support from mentors or peers, and staying focused on the long-term benefits of vulnerability.

Moreover, effective communication plays a crucial role in overcoming challenges and resistance. Leaders should regularly communicate the importance of vulnerability, explain its impact on trust and collaboration, and address team members' concerns or doubts. Open and transparent communication helps foster understanding and paves the way for acceptance and adoption of vulnerability in leadership.

By acknowledging and addressing challenges and resistance, leaders can create an environment where vulnerability is embraced and valued. Over time, with persistence and consistent effort, vulnerability can become a powerful tool for building trust, fostering collaboration, and driving positive organizational change.

Developing Vulnerability as a Leadership Skill:

Vulnerability is a natural human trait and a powerful leadership skill that can enhance relationships, build trust, and drive success. Leaders who wish to cultivate vulnerability can follow practical tips and techniques to develop this skill and create a more open and authentic leadership style.

Foster Self-Awareness: Developing vulnerability starts with understanding oneself. Leaders should engage in introspection and self-reflection to gain insight into their emotions, strengths, and weaknesses. By becoming more self-aware, leaders can identify areas where they can be more open and vulnerable in their interactions with others.

Embrace Authenticity: Authenticity is at the core of vulnerability. Leaders should strive to be genuine, allowing their team members to see their authentic selves. This can involve sharing personal stories, expressing feelings and thoughts openly, and admitting mistakes when they occur. Authenticity helps build trust and creates an environment where others feel comfortable being vulnerable.

Encourage Open Communication: Leaders can foster vulnerability by creating a culture of open communication. Encourage team members to share their thoughts, ideas, and concerns openly. Actively listen and show empathy towards their perspectives. Creating a safe space for open dialogue allows leaders to inspire others to be more vulnerable in expressing their thoughts and feelings.

Practice Active Feedback: Providing and receiving feedback is an opportunity for vulnerability. Leaders should actively seek feedback from their team members and demonstrate openness to criticism or suggestions. This creates an environment where constructive feedback is valued and encourages others to be vulnerable in sharing their insights.

Commit to Continuous Improvement: Like any skill, vulnerability requires continuous effort and improvement. Leaders should commit to personal growth and embrace vulnerability as an ongoing journey. They should seek learning opportunities, attend workshops or seminars, and engage in self-development practices that promote vulnerability.

Leaders can develop vulnerability as a leadership skill by following these tips and techniques. It takes practice, self-awareness, and a commitment to continuous improvement. As leaders become more comfortable with vulnerability, they create an environment where authenticity, trust, and collaboration flourish, leading to increased team engagement and overall organizational success.

At this point, where do you stand?

Therefore, vulnerability in leadership plays a crucial role in creating psychological safety and driving workplace innovation. By embracing vulnerability, leaders foster trust, encourage open communication, and build stronger relationships with their team members. This, in turn, creates an environment where individuals feel safe to take risks, share ideas, and contribute to innovation and growth. The ability to overcome challenges and resistance associated with vulnerability allows leaders to lead with resilience and authenticity. Developing vulnerability as a leadership skill requires self-awareness, a commitment to continuous improvement, and an emphasis on creating a culture of trust and open communication. Ultimately, vulnerability in leadership sets the stage for psychological safety, enabling teams to thrive and organizations to achieve tremendous success through innovation. [60]

5.5 Embracing Vulnerability as a Lifestyle: Living Boldly

"Wabi-Sabi is the beauty of things imperfect, impermanent, and incomplete, the antithesis of our classical Western notion of beauty as something perfect, enduring, and monumental."
Leonard Koren

In Japan, there is a concept known as "***wabi-sabi***."
It is a celebration of the value of imperfection.
It sees the cracks and flaws as something to be treasured – rather than something to fix or address.
While introspecting my life over the past sixty years, I discovered my most important feature: I am "imperfect" regarding all the social markers people use to evaluate and judge me. At that time, I came across Japan's "Wabi-Subi" concept.
I do not blame anyone. I have always spoken up. Instead, I was outspoken; whether right or wrong, I have had an opinion on any issue worldwide and made it public. As a result, they discarded me and distanced themselves from me. I no longer exist in their life with all possible labels on me. I do not think my tiny body can accommodate any more labels.
I was not a good communicator then, and I do not know how good I am today. However, I continue to talk in known or unknown gatherings/places, whether at formal places like banks, colleges, or corporate offices or with the tea seller, co-passengers in train/bus/ metro/ social media, or morning walkers wherever I may stay.
The difference between then and now is that I create many posts on my insights and publish them on blog medium.com/ LinkedIn/ YouTube, as well as other social media, including

WhatsApp, where people give their opinions somewhat as they fit. I find it enjoyable as I engage with them primarily digitally but sometimes by directly talking to them.

Since October 2023, I have been writing books and doing the same with profound studies and research, which I am publishing one after another. This is the fifth book in the nonfiction category of self-help. I hope to publish as many books as possible until I live and become an authority globally. I love to dream and continue to march through ups and downs, failures and successes.

I was elated with the idea of "Wabi-Sabi."

I discovered that this idea of celebrating imperfection extended to more than just an ornately repaired bowl or a chipped wooden table. It resonated across everything. Work, personal and professional relationships, health...I could see the value of wabi-sabi everywhere.

Let us be honest: We are obsessed with being perfect

This chase for perfection can be toxic. It causes us to act out of a place of fear in everything we do, whether it is public speaking or the need to say and do the right thing in front of others. Moreover, left unchecked, it can lead to even more significant mental health challenges like imposter syndrome, anxiety, or depression.

Here is the thing, though: We are NOT perfect

Nobody—not you, me, or anyone else—is perfect. Not by a long shot. Not even the person you know who always dresses on point appears unnecessarily intelligent and is good at everything.

We all have made mistakes and will continue to make mistakes. We will say the wrong things, do the wrong things, disappoint people, and disappoint ourselves. It is all part of being human.

When you recognize that nobody is perfect, it is incredibly liberating. It takes the pressure off needing to be the best and never failing, giving you the courage and space to grow, create more profound and meaningful relationships, and embrace more experiences.

So, in celebration of imperfection and wabi-sabi, here are five stories of people who embraced their vulnerability, mistakes, and flaws—and emerged much stronger for it.

Brené Brown and the power of vulnerability:

I cannot talk about imperfection without mentioning Brené Brown.

A researcher and a storyteller, Brené delivered a game-changing TED talk in 2010 about the power of vulnerability, which has since been viewed more than 58 million times. In her talk, Brene speaks about how her desire to research human connection led her on a personal path to embrace her vulnerability.

Raised in a ***"suck it up and get it done"*** family, Brene spent years trying to outrun her imperfections and outsmart her vulnerability—causing her to try and make everything in life specific. When she started conducting her academic research, she set out to understand and quantify human connection in tangible terms. To organize it into a "***code***" for everyone to see. After speaking to thousands of people, Brene had folders of stories about connection and disconnection. However, only one variable separated the people with a strong sense of love and connection from those who struggled for it: the former believed they were worthy of belonging.

When she dug even more deeply, she found two common threads in the first group:

They had a sense of courage and bravery, and

They embraced vulnerability.

As someone who had rejected vulnerability her whole life, Brene had a "little breakdown" (her words, not mine). She spent the next couple of years trying to understand her struggle with vulnerability and quickly discovered that she was not alone.

Everyone out there was trying to hide their vulnerable side. They were scared to ask for help. They were scared to show weakness or imperfection. They were scared of not having all the answers. Moreover, this fear led to a society where people blame others, try to fix every flaw, act out of fear, and avoid pain.

What became even more apparent to Brene is that in numbing our vulnerability, we also numbed ourselves to joy, gratitude, and happiness.

This led Brene to change the way she thought about vulnerability thoroughly. Instead of rejecting imperfection, she challenged her perceptions, embraced them, and called on others worldwide to do the same. Unsurprisingly, her story of vulnerability has resonated with millions worldwide and led countless people to change their thinking, from Oprah to Tim Ferris.

"To let ourselves be seen, deeply seen, vulnerably seen ... to love with our whole hearts, even though there is no guarantee—and that is hard, and I can tell you as a parent, that is excruciatingly difficult—to practice gratitude and joy in those moments of

terror when we are wondering, 'Can I love you this much? Can I believe in this passionately? Can I be this fierce about this?' just to be able to stop and, instead of catastrophizing what might happen, to say, 'I am just so grateful because to feel this vulnerable means I am alive.' Moreover, the last, which I think is probably the most important, is believing we are enough. Because when we work from a place, I believe, that says, 'I am enough' … then we stop screaming and start listening, we are kinder and gentler to the people around us, and we are kinder and gentler to ourselves."

—Brene Brown

"Have no fear of perfection—you will never reach it. So said the artist Salvador Dali, who created surrealist masterpieces without worrying too much about whether they were just right. If he had waited for perfection, he would never have picked up a paintbrush."

- ***Sir Richard Branson***

Sir Richard Branson's tale of overcoming the odds:

I am not the only fan of Sir Richard Branson, and for good reason. The British billionaire has had just a few successes in life, including founding the mega-successful Virgin Group, making the Time 100 Most Influential People in the World list, and being the third oldest person to fly to space.

<u>However, I did not know that Richard Branson had dyslexia.</u>

When Branson was in school, he struggled to follow what was happening. He dropped out at age 15 and created multiple businesses before founding Virgin Records in the 1970s. As his business grew, Branson learned to focus on his strengths, admit his shortcomings, and delegate tasks to others. This meant owning his flaws and trusting others to do a lot of the reading, writing, and accounting while he focused on the creative and strategic side of the business.

Surprisingly, this has been a massive part of Virgin's success. Branson would have others read the company's marketing materials back to him, and he would only keep those he could understand quickly. This meant that everything Virgin put out was sharp, easy to understand, and highly memorable.

Even though he continually adds to his meteoric list of achievements, Richard Branson remains open about his weaknesses. He is unafraid to be vulnerable and puts his imperfections on the table, using them to make his team stronger by hiring people who complement his abilities. [61]

5.6:10 Main Takeaways: Vulnerability: The Gateway to Resilience and Authenticity

1. **Embrace Vulnerability for Growth**: Vulnerability is not a weakness but a catalyst for personal and professional growth. Leaders like Howard Schultz demonstrate that sharing vulnerabilities fosters authenticity and

strengthens connections, which is essential for inspiring teams and driving innovation.

2. **Authenticity Drives Leadership**: Inspiring leaders prioritize authenticity over perfection. Sharing personal stories and treating employees benevolently builds trust and creates a supportive work environment conducive to success.
3. **Courageous Leadership**: Effective leadership requires courage to confront uncertainties and risks. Leaders encouraging openness and emotional exposure empower their teams to innovate and excel.
4. **Resilience and Grit Matter**: As Jensen Huang of Nvidia emphasizes, resilience and grit often trump academic pedigree in predicting success. Facing adversity builds character and prepares individuals for challenges in the workplace.
5. **Navigating Conflict with Vulnerability**: In relationships and conflicts, embracing vulnerability facilitates understanding and resolution. Acknowledging emotions and needs fosters healthier interactions and helps in navigating disputes constructively.
6. **Embrace Vulnerability**: Vulnerability in relationships, leadership, and personal growth is crucial for building trust and fostering genuine connections. It involves being authentic, transparent, and open about emotions and imperfections.
7. **Choose Love Over Fear**: Operating from a place of love rather than fear transforms relationships. Choosing acceptance over judgment creates a supportive

environment where both partners can grow together, communicate openly, and resolve conflicts constructively.

8. **Leadership and Vulnerability**: Effective leadership involves embracing vulnerability to create psychological safety within teams. Authentic and humble leaders inspire trust, encourage innovation, and empower their teams to take risks and learn from mistakes.
9. **Overcoming Perfectionism**: The pursuit of perfection can be detrimental. Embracing imperfection (wabi-sabi) allows individuals to grow, form deeper connections, and find joy in life's uncertainties without fearing failure or judgment.
10. **Learning from Role Models**: Examples like Brené Brown and Richard Branson highlight the power of vulnerability in personal and professional success. Their stories underscore how embracing vulnerability can lead to resilience, creativity, and meaningful achievements.

Book Summary

Chapter 1: Unconventional Wisdom: Embrace Your Truth- 10 Main Takeaways

1. **Embrace Failure as a Learning Tool:** The story of the Taj Mahal and Richard Branson highlights how failure can be a stepping stone to success. The author faced 50 manuscript rejections, while Branson struggled with dyslexia and ADHD, demonstrating that repeated failures can lead to eventual success.
2. **Challenge Conventional Wisdom:** The Taj Mahal, often seen as a love symbol, can also be viewed as a monument of misplaced priorities during famine. Questioning accepted narratives can lead to deeper understanding and personal growth.
3. **Understand Your Unique Perspective:** Personal perspectives are subjective and valuable, like views on a half-full or half-empty glass. Recognizing and valuing your unique viewpoint helps you navigate life holistically.
4. **Right to Make Mistakes:** Accepting and learning from mistakes is crucial. Making independent decisions and owning outcomes fosters growth more effectively than following others' advice, which may not suit your unique situation.
5. **Self-Belief Over Social Expectations**: Society imposes limiting beliefs, especially on those with ADHD or dyslexia. Overcoming negative perceptions and believing in your potential is essential for personal success.

6. **Critique of Social Judgments**: Negative judgments faced by individuals with learning differences highlight the need for a more inclusive society. Emphasizing neurodiverse strengths fosters compassion and understanding.
7. **Impact of Historical Actions on Present Perceptions:** The Taj Mahal's construction during a famine shows how past actions shape current perceptions. Understanding this context forms nuanced opinions about historical symbols.
8. **Value of Independent Thinking**: Independent thinking is crucial for personal growth. Developing the courage to think and act independently leads to authentic and fulfilling life choices.
9. **Redefining Success and Worth:** Success should be measured by personal growth and learning, not societal benchmarks. The author's and Branson's experiences show that perceived failures can lead to significant achievements and self-discovery.
10. **Power of Vulnerability:** Embracing vulnerability is a powerful tool for personal development. Confronting weaknesses and fears builds resilience and self-understanding, leading to a more authentic and empowered life.

Chapter 2: Shifting Perspectives: Understanding the Power of Mindset- 10 Main Takeaways

1. **The Power of an Open Stance and Vulnerability:** Embracing openness and vulnerability fuels personal growth. Ramana Rao advocates stepping beyond comfort zones to embrace new experiences, fostering curiosity and learning. Gus Worland underscores vulnerability's role in breaking barriers and facilitating emotional growth and connection.
2. **Cultivating Resilience:** Nidhi Tewari emphasizes resilience through discomfort. Growth across emotional, mental, spiritual, and physical realms builds resilience, vital for overcoming challenges and achieving enduring success.
3. **Leading with Curiosity:** Eric Liu champions curiosity-driven leadership. Questioning beliefs fosters continuous learning and openness, which is pivotal for personal and communal growth.
4. **The Impact of Mindset on Success**: Henry Ford and Carol S. Dweck state that Mindset shapes success. A growth mindset views challenges as opportunities, fostering perseverance and adaptability toward achieving goals.
5. **Breaking Free from Limiting Beliefs**: John Fullbright's tale highlights overcoming limiting beliefs. Challenging such beliefs unlocks potential, enabling remarkable personal growth and achievement.
6. **Clarify Your Goals:** Start by defining a specific goal clearly and understand why you want to achieve it. The more precise your vision, the easier it becomes to visualize success.

7. **Practice Mental Rehearsal:** Adopt athletes' 'Mental Rehearsal' technique. Imagine yourself achieving your goal in vivid detail, engaging all senses. This daily practice reinforces your commitment and enhances performance.
8. **Create a Vision Board:** Use a vision board with images and words that represent your goals achieved. This visual reminder keeps your aspirations tangible and reinforces motivation.
9. **Use Affirmations:** Use positive affirmations that affirm your goals as already achieved. This helps maintain focus, boost confidence, and align your subconscious with your objectives.
10. **Live in the Moment:** Balance visualization with present-moment awareness. Regularly review and visualize your goals, then release them and focus on present actions. This practice enhances clarity and effectiveness in daily tasks.

Chapter 3: Self-Compassion: Cultivating Emotional Intelligence for Success- 10 Main Takeaways

1. **Emotional Intelligence (EI) Beyond IQ:** Jeffrey Skilling and Kenneth Lay lacked emotional intelligence despite their high IQs, leading to their downfall at Enron. EI involves understanding and managing emotions effectively, which is crucial for making wise decisions and avoiding costly mistakes in personal and professional life.
2. **Components of EI:** EI comprises self-awareness, self-regulation, motivation, empathy, and social skills. These

components empower individuals to navigate challenges, manage stress, build relationships, and focus on long-term goals rather than short-term gains.

3. **Self-Regulation**: Mastering self-regulation allows individuals to control impulses, manage negative emotions like anger, and respond thoughtfully rather than impulsively. This skill is essential for effective leadership and personal growth.
4. **Practical Strategies**: Techniques like mindfulness, self-reflection, and recognizing physiological cues can help enhance self-awareness and self-regulation, contributing to overall emotional intelligence.
5. **Benefits of EI**: Research indicates that EI is more predictive of success than IQ in various life domains, including academic achievement, career advancement, and personal relationships. Investing in EI development can improve decision-making, interpersonal skills, and overall well-being.
6. **Professional and Personal Success**: EI is a critical skill for success across various fields, enhancing resilience, social skills, and leadership effectiveness. Research underscores its role in better job performance, stress management, and fostering positive workplace relationships.
7. **Relationships and Communication**: High EI fosters better interpersonal relations by improving empathy, conflict resolution, and communication. Individuals with higher EI are adept at managing emotions, which enhances their ability to connect meaningfully with others.

8. **Stress Management**: EI equips individuals with tools to recognize and manage stress effectively, improving mental and physical well-being. This skill is crucial in high-pressure environments like workplaces.
9. **Decision-Making and Motivation**: EI enhances decision-making by helping individuals manage emotional interference. It also boosts intrinsic motivation, which is vital for achieving personal and professional goals.
10. **Happiness and Well-Being**: Emotional intelligence significantly improves self-awareness, relationship satisfaction, and stress reduction, enhancing life satisfaction and well-being.

Chapter 4: Rewiring Your Brain: Unraveling the Neuroscience of Change-10 Main Takeaways:

1. **Neuroplasticity and Mindset Shifts:** Understanding neuroplasticity allows individuals to reframe their thoughts and behaviors by actively rewiring their brains. Techniques such as relabeling negative thoughts, identifying their source, and refocusing attention positively can facilitate lasting behavioral changes.
2. **Practical Strategies for Enhancing Neuroplasticity**: Daily nutrition, adequate sleep, and mental exercises (e.g., using the non-dominant hand and learning new skills) can strengthen neural pathways and improve cognitive flexibility and performance.
3. **Impact of Dopamine and Serotonin**: Recognizing the roles of dopamine in motivation and serotonin in mood

regulation underscores their importance in mental well-being. Balanced levels of these neurotransmitters through lifestyle adjustments can enhance happiness and productivity.

4. **Biological Basis of Happiness**: Happiness involves complex biological and environmental factors interplay. Genetic predispositions and brain chemistry significantly influence one's ability to experience and sustain happiness.
5. **Practical Applications in Daily Life:** Integrating mindfulness practices, maintaining a healthy lifestyle, and fostering positive social connections can optimize brain function, promote emotional resilience, and enhance overall life satisfaction.
6. **Understanding Habit Formation:** Habits are behaviors repeated regularly and subconsciously, influenced by cues and rewards. To develop good habits like exercise or healthier eating, simplify the process and make it enjoyable, such as exercising with a friend or prepping easy meals. Breaking bad habits involves identifying triggers and substituting them with healthier alternatives supported by a supportive environment.
7. **Challenges in Habit Development**: Initial effort, consistency, and the lure of instant gratification are common hurdles in forming good habits. Overambitious goals and a lack of patience can lead to setbacks. It is crucial to start small, practice early in the day, and repeat consistently to override brain resistance.
8. The Role of Brain-Based Learning in Habit Formation: Brain-based learning, a method that enhances retention by engaging multiple senses and teaching others what you

have learned, plays a significant role in habit formation. Relating new information to previous knowledge, gaining practical experience, and using testing to reinforce learning are all effective strategies. Understanding your unique learning style and avoiding multitasking also promote effective learning.

9. **Practical Strategies for Lasting Change**: Recognize triggers for bad habits, gradually replace routines, and maintain progress by tracking behavior. Setting realistic goals and understanding motivation are crucial to breaking bad habits and fostering good ones.
10. **Creating Supportive Environments:** Foster an environment conducive to positive habits by leveraging tools like habit-tracking apps and setting clear goals. Building a supportive social circle and cultivating willpower through mindfulness and self-control techniques enhance habit formation

Chapter 5: Vulnerability: The Gateway to Resilience and Authenticity- 10 Main Takeaways:

1. **Embrace Vulnerability for Growth**: Vulnerability is not a weakness but a catalyst for personal and professional growth. Leaders like Howard Schultz demonstrate that sharing vulnerabilities fosters authenticity and strengthens connections, which is essential for inspiring teams and driving innovation.
2. **Authenticity Drives Leadership**: Inspiring leaders prioritize authenticity over perfection. Sharing personal

stories and treating employees benevolently builds trust and creates a supportive work environment conducive to success.

3. **Courageous Leadership**: Effective leadership requires courage to confront uncertainties and risks. Leaders encouraging openness and emotional exposure empower their teams to innovate and excel.
4. **Resilience and Grit Matter**: As Jensen Huang of Nvidia emphasizes, resilience and grit often trump academic pedigree in predicting success. Facing adversity builds character and prepares individuals for challenges in the workplace.
5. **Navigating Conflict with Vulnerability**: In relationships and conflicts, embracing vulnerability facilitates understanding and resolution. Acknowledging emotions and needs fosters healthier interactions and helps in navigating disputes constructively.
6. **Embrace Vulnerability**: Vulnerability in relationships, leadership, and personal growth is crucial for building trust and fostering genuine connections. It involves being authentic, transparent, and open about emotions and imperfections.
7. **Choose Love Over Fear**: Operating from a place of love rather than fear transforms relationships. Choosing acceptance over judgment creates a supportive environment where both partners can grow together, communicate openly, and resolve conflicts constructively.
8. **Leadership and Vulnerability**: Effective leadership involves embracing vulnerability to create psychological safety within teams. Authentic and humble leaders inspire

trust, encourage innovation, and empower their teams to take risks and learn from mistakes.

9. **Overcoming Perfectionism**: The pursuit of perfection can be detrimental. Embracing imperfection (wabi-sabi) allows individuals to grow, form deeper connections, and find joy in life's uncertainties without fearing failure or judgment.
10. **Learning from Role Models**: Examples like Brené Brown and Richard Branson highlight the power of vulnerability in personal and professional success. Their stories underscore how embracing vulnerability can lead to resilience, creativity, and meaningful achievements.

Conclusion

"Dare Your Vulnerability" invites you on a transformative journey, urging you to embrace your true self, shift your mindset, cultivate emotional intelligence, harness the power of your brain, and recognize the strength in vulnerability. As you explore these themes, you will find practical wisdom and inspiring stories illustrating the profound impact of daring to be vulnerable.

Chapter 1: Unconventional Wisdom: Embrace Your Truth

In Chapter 1 you will learn to see failure as a stepping stone to success. Through the tales of the Taj Mahal and Richard Branson, you are encouraged to question conventional wisdom and recognize your unique perspective. This chapter emphasizes self-belief over societal expectations, encouraging you to value independent thinking and redefine success on your terms. ***By embracing your truth, you pave the way for personal growth and fulfillment.***

Chapter 2: Shifting Perspectives: Understanding the Power of Mindset

Chapter 2 emphasizes the transformative power of an open stance and vulnerability. By fostering resilience, leading with curiosity, and breaking free from limiting beliefs, you can discover the impact of mindset on success. ***Practical strategies such as mental rehearsal, creating a vision board, and using affirmations are presented***

to help you clarify and achieve your goals. Shifting your mindset empowers you to see opportunities where others see obstacles, leading to a more fulfilling and successful life.

Chapter 3: Self-Compassion: Cultivating Emotional Intelligence for Success

Chapter 3 highlights the importance of emotional intelligence (EI) in personal and professional life. Enhancing self-awareness, self-regulation, motivation, empathy, and social skills enables you to navigate challenges more effectively. This chapter provides practical strategies for improving EI, highlighting its benefits in decision-making, stress management, and fostering meaningful relationships. ***Cultivating emotional intelligence allows you to connect deeply with others and lead a balanced, emotionally healthy life.***

Chapter 4: Rewiring Your Brain: Unraveling the Neuroscience of Change

Chapter 4 delves into the science of neuroplasticity and how you can reframe your thoughts and behaviors. You will learn about the roles of dopamine and serotonin in motivation and mood regulation and practical strategies to enhance neuroplasticity. ***Understanding habit formation and leveraging brain-based learning techniques will empower you to create lasting, positive changes in your life. By rewiring your brain, you can break free from old patterns and create a more productive, joyful future.***

Chapter 5: Vulnerability: The Gateway to Resilience and Authenticity

Chapter 5 explores how embracing vulnerability can lead to growth, resilience, and authenticity. You will build trust and foster a supportive environment by sharing personal stories and practicing courageous leadership. This chapter emphasizes the importance of overcoming perfectionism and choosing love over fear, highlighting the profound impact of vulnerability on personal and professional success. ***Embracing vulnerability allows you to live more authentically and connect deeply with others, fostering a more prosperous, more meaningful life.***

Why You Should Read "Dare Your Vulnerability"?

"Dare Your Vulnerability" is a compelling guide for anyone looking to unlock their full potential and live a more authentic, empowered life. The book's practical takeaways and inspiring stories will resonate with readers from all walks of life. Whether striving for personal growth, professional success, or deeper connections, this book provides the tools and insights to embrace your true self and navigate life's challenges with courage and resilience.

By purchasing "Dare Your Vulnerability," you take the first step towards self-discovery and empowerment. The lessons within will not only transform how you view yourself but also how you interact with the world around you. Embrace this opportunity to learn, grow, and thrive by daring to be vulnerable.

Conclusion

In conclusion, "Dare Your Vulnerability" is more than just a book; it is a roadmap to a more fulfilling and authentic life. By embracing your vulnerabilities, shifting your mindset, cultivating emotional intelligence, and rewiring your brain, you will discover the power within you to achieve extraordinary things. Take the leap and dare your vulnerability today—your future self will thank you.

My best wishes,

Author

Sekhar Kumar Dey

References

1. **Kinra, Rajeev (2015). Writing Self, Writing Empire: Chandar Bhan Brahman and the Cultural World of the Indo-Persian State Secretary. Oakland: University of California Press.**
2. **Mumtaz Mahal. (2024, May 7). In Wikipedia.** https://en.wikipedia.org/wiki/Mumtaz_Mahal
3. https://en.wikipedia.org/wiki/Deccan_famine_of_1630%E2%80%931632
4. https://indiancoins.com/product/mughal-akbar-mahmudi-coinage-silver-mahmudi-mulher-mint-sp-462/
5. https://famineanddearth.exeter.ac.uk/aboutthemap.html
6. https://en.wikipedia.org/wiki/Richard_Branson
7. https://www.madebydyslexia.org/
8. https://www.linkedin.com/pulse/ask-richard-stage-your-life-what-motivates-you-richard-branson-wjwrc/?trackingId=XTiwptZzluWmRhM4bEp5MQ%3D%3D
9. https://www.lawinfo.com/resources/criminal-defense/what-is-blackstone-s-formulation-in-criminal.html

10. https://www.linkedin.com/pulse/day-2-ted2024-discovery-growth-ted-conferences-bup4e/?trackingId=GkoviQOzSLKNrte%2F83a1mw%3D%3D
11. http://www.ted.com
12. https://www.linkedin.com/in/ramanarao/
13. https://www.linkedin.com/in/gus-worland-577705152/
14. https://www.linkedin.com/in/nidhitewarilcsw/
15. https://www.linkedin.com/in/eric-liu-182655/
16. https://www.linkedin.com/feed/update/urn:li:ugcPost:7186205030058795009?commentUrn=urn%3Ali%3Acomment%3A%28ugcPost%3A7186205030058795009%2C7186425619121946624%29&dashCommentUrn=urn%3Ali%3Afsd_comment%3A%287186425619121946624%2Curn%3Ali%3AugcPost%3A7186205030058795009%29
17. https://www.linkedin.com/in/john-fullbright-a0a80115a?utm_source=share&utm_campaign=share_via&utm_content=profile&utm_medium=android_app
18. https://medium.com/@hawkeyes108sk/fail-more-fail-fast-a0f33c15efcd
19. https://exploringyourmind.com/how-does-your-mindset-influence-your-success/
20. https://exploringyourmind.com/how-does-your-mindset-influence-your-success/

21. https://innerlightjournal.com/overcome-your-limiting-beliefs/
22. https://www.positivelykimberly.com/visualization-intention/
23. https://a.co/d/3DqafMr
24. https://jackcanfield.com/blog/visualization-techniques-manifest-your-dreams/#:~:text=By%20writing%20down%20your%20goals,person%20in%20your%20life%20%E2%80%94%20YOU!
25. https://hbr.org/2021/01/the-secret-to-building-resilience
26. https://lightloveandlevity.com/self-care-mantras-as-daily-routine/
27. https://qr.ae/psevbR
28. https://www.mdpi.com/2076-328X/8/5/45
29. https://www.amazon.com/The-Smartest-Guys-Room-Scandalous/dp/1591840538
30. https://www.quora.com/What-are-some-inspiring-short-stories-on-emotional-intelligence
31. https://positivepsychology.com/importance-of-emotional-intelligence/#hero-single
32. https://www.breakthrough-experience.co.uk/post/the-neuroscience-of-transformation
33. https://www.americanexpress.com/en-us/business/trends-and-insights/articles/the-neuroscience-of-changeor-how-to-reset-your-brain/

34. https://www.americanexpress.com/en-us/business/trends-and-insights/articles/the-neuroscience-of-changeor-how-to-reset-your-brain/
35. https://www.bbc.com/future/article/20230912-how-i-hacked-my-brain
36. https://www.mindshine.app/
37. https://www.europeanceo.com/business-and-management/to-become-a-better-leader-look-to-neuroscience/
38. https://www.verywellhealth.com/memory-tip-1-keyword-mnemonics-98466
39. https://www.withinmeditation.com/within-work
40. https://www.atlassian.com/blog/productivity/neuroplasticity-train-your-brain
41. https://www.verywellmind.com/what-is-happiness-4869755
42. https://iaap-journals.onlinelibrary.wiley.com/doi/10.1111/j.1758-0854.2009.01008.x
43. https://www.ncbi.nlm.nih.gov/pmc/articles/PMC4449495/
44. https://www.medicalnewstoday.com/articles/326090
45. https://www.verywellmind.com/what-is-maslows-hierarchy-of-needs-4136760

46. https://www.verywellmind.com/what-is-happiness-4869755#citation-7
47. https://qr.ae/psJrn4
48. https://www.quora.com/Why-is-it-so-hard-to-develop-and-maintain-good-habits?no_redirect=1
49. https://cognitiontoday.com/brain-based-learning-theory-strategies-and-concepts/
50. https://www.forbes.com/sites/carminegallo/2016/12/02/how-starbucks-ceo-howard-schultz-inspired-us-to-dream-bigger/
51. https://www.linkedin.com/pulse/dispelling-myths-vulnerability-terra-carter/
52. https://www.forbes.com/sites/jackkelly/2024/04/01/i-hope-suffering-happens-to-you-hiring-for-grit-over-pedigree/
53. https://www.dorlitablakely.com/healing/embracing-vulnerability-the-key-to-authenticity-and-personal-growth/
54. https://www.gottman.com/blog/choose-love-over-fear/
55. https://the-conflictexpert.com/2019/08/22/being-vulnerable-can-resolve-conflict-heres-how/
56. https://the-conflictexpert.com/2019/08/22/being-vulnerable-can-resolve-conflict-heres-how/

57. https://www.gottman.com/blog/choose-love-over-fear/
58. https://www.quora.com/What-are-the-benefits-of-emotional-vulnerability-in-relationships/answer/Patrick-Holley-M-Div-LPCC-S-Holley-Counseling?ch=3&oid=389490360&share=5feb1b9c&srid=uRN51g&target_type=answer
59. https://www.thehrdigest.com/vulnerability-in-leadership-why-being-human-is-good-for-business/
60. https://www.leaderfactor.com/learn/vulnerability-in-leadership
61. https://www.thevectorimpact.com/stories-of-vulnerability/

Disclaimer

This book is for educational purposes only. Readers acknowledge that the author does not render legal, financial, medical, or professional advice. The content of the book has been derived from various sources. Please consult a licensed professional advice before attempting any techniques outlined in this book.

By reading this document, the reader agrees that under no circumstances is the author responsible for any direct or indirect losses incurred due to the use of the information contained within this document, including but not limited to errors, omissions, or inaccuracies. Adherence to all applicable laws and regulations, including international, federal, state, and local governing professional licensing, business practices, advertising, and all other jurisdictions, is the sole responsibility of the purchaser or reader.

Neither the author nor the publisher assumes any responsibility or liability on behalf of the purchaser or reader of these materials. Any perceived slight of any individual or organization is purely unintentional.

Your Voice Matters: May I ask you for a small favor?

Honored Readers,

First, I want to thank you for reading this book. You could have chosen any other book, but you took mine, and I appreciate this.

I hope this message finds you healthy and happy as you read these lines. I am incredibly grateful as I write this letter and reflect on the travels we have experienced together within the pages of my book, "Dare Your Vulnerability." Your everlasting faith in me and unfailing encouragement have given me valuable motivation and approval.

Your suggestions are essential to my creative process as an independent scribe. They fuel my passion and allow me to go deeply into the core of my creative attempts and find the heart of my writing. I respectfully ask that you consider posting a review for "Dare Your Vulnerability" to gain valuable insights and opinions.

Your review does not need to be in-depth or extensive; even a brief collection of ideas that expresses your true feelings will do. Whether your comments are compliments or constructive criticism, they are all essential building blocks in my search for ongoing development as a writer and storyteller.

Your review has more impact than words on a screen because it can influence potential customers and direct them on their literary journeys. Your advice essentially serves as a lighthouse, guiding me as I embark on new literary endeavors.

I implore you to set aside some of your valuable time to express your opinions in online journals or sites like Amazon, Goodreads, or whichever digital harbor serves as your entryway to my creative universe. By working together to ignite the spark of creativity in the hearts and brains of countless people, we can further strengthen our symbiotic relationship as readers and creators.

Please accept my sincere appreciation for your involvement in this literary journey. I am looking forward to the chance to share more stories that speak to the core of your minds and souls, and I am also looking forward to your upcoming reviews with great enthusiasm.

Keeping it straight – reviews are the lifeblood of any author.

Sincere regards,

(Sekhar Kumar Dey)

www.ingramcontent.com/pod-product-compliance
Lightning Source LLC
LaVergne TN
LVHW052321200926
848481LV00002B/630